Husserl and Heidegger

SUNY Series in Philosophy
Robert C. Neville, Editor

Husserl and Heidegger: The Question of a Phenomenological Beginning

Timothy J. Stapleton

State University of New York Press
Albany

142.7

S⊥ 2h

127850

mar. 1984

Published by
State University of New York Press, Albany

© 1983 State University of New York

All rights reserved

Printed in the United States of America

For information, address State University of New York Press, State University Plaza, Albany, N.Y., 12246

Library of Congress Cataloging in Publication Data

Stapleton, Timothy J., 1951–
  Husserl and Heidegger.

  (SUNY series in philosophy)
  Includes bibliographical references and index.
  1. Husserl, Edmund, 1859–1938. 2. Heidegger, Martin, 1889–1976. 3. Phenomenology—History. I. Title. II. Series.
  B3279.H94S7 1983   142'.7   83–412
  ISBN 0-87395-744-X
  ISBN 0-87395-745-8 (pbk.)
   10 9 8 7 6 5 4 3 2 1

FOR MY MOTHER AND FATHER

Contents

Acknowledgments

I owe a special debt of gratitude to Joseph Kockelmans of The Pennsylvania State University, whose advice, encouragement, and timely criticism proved so valuable in the early stages of this project. I also want to thank the editors of *Man and World* for allowing me to use a version of Chapter 3 that was published in that journal under the title, "The Logic of the Transcendental Reduction."

Introduction
The Nature of the Problem

ERLEAU-PONTY, IN THE Preface to *The Phenomenology of Perception*, remarked on the curiosity of having to ask the question "What is phenomenology?" some fifty years after the movement's inception in Husserl's first writings. And even today, the question still persists. In part this is due to the fact that for most phenomenologists their method or mode of reflection is identical with philosophy itself. From such a perspective, the question "What is phenomenology?" is the same as the question "What is philosophy?" The latter question is much older, its origin coinciding with the birth of philosophy. For it seems indigenous to the philosophical enterprise that, in the spirit of critical self-awareness, it examine its own nature. Hence, as long as philosophy remains true to its origins, this question must persist.

But this only partially accounts for the uncertainty or hesitation about the meaning of phenomenological philosophy. For we can still ask what it means to pursue philosophy phenomenologically. What is it that constitutes a *phenomenological* attempt at self-understanding? How does phenomenology try to understand itself in a process internal to itself? The history of the phenomenological movement, however, seems to make a single or unified answer to these questions impossible, for the unity underlying the diverse philosophical projects customarily labelled "phenomenological," the one in the many, proves singularly resistant to our inquiring gaze.

That the works of Edmund Husserl mark the birth of phenomenology in the contemporary sense is generally recognized. Philosophers as diverse as Scheler, Ingarden, Heidegger, Sartre, Merleau-Ponty, and Gadamer, all view Husserl as the father of phenomenology. Yet none of these thinkers can be said actually to have carried out a phenomenological program consistent with the fundamental tenets of Husserlian phenomenology. They are indeed autonomous thinkers who recognize their debt to Husserl, but for whom the label of "disciple" is totally inadequate. But over and beyond their stature as independent thinkers, with their own problems and creative insights, there persists a most fundamental objection to the way in which Husserl's philosophy developed. And perhaps more than any other facet of Husserlian phenomenology, it is the transcendental turn to an *absolute consciousness*, the articulation of a *transcendental idealism*, which provides a common point of opposition among these individuals.

The directions from which these objections are launched, however, have been varied. The Göttingen and Munich schools insist upon a phenomenological realism, as opposed to a phenomenological idealism. French phenomenologists such as Sartre and Merleau-Ponty have developed an existential phenomenology. And both Heidegger, in his phenomenological stage, along with Gadamer claim that phenomenology must be hermeneutic rather than transcendental. Husserl, on the other hand, always insists that any philosophy which fails to effect the transcendental reduction violates the basic phenomenological maxim, "*Zu Sachen selbst!*" ("To the things themselves!"). And yet, for all intents and purposes, Husserl stands alone as the exponent of a transcendental phenomenology. This state of affairs offers a most serious challenge to the unity of the phenomenological project. It is not simply a difference in temperament or in interests, but in the essence of phenomenology itself.

To show how these different positions developed, to reveal the nature of the issues which fostered this diversity, and to uncover a unitary sense of phenomenology which guides all of these authors, is a task which exceeds the bounds of this study. What will be attempted, instead, is to focus upon one part of this complex question, that of the relationship between the phenomenologies of Husserl and the early Heidegger (1927–29). Heidegger's dedication of *Being and Time* to Husserl, his thanks for Husserl's making available unpublished manuscripts,[1] and his praise of the *Logical Investigations*,[2] testify to the dependency, in Heidegger's view at least, of his own philosophical development on the phenomenology of Husserl. And yet despite such clues, the entire approach of *Being and Time* must strike the reader as so foreign to that of Husserl that the nature of this dependency, and of the relations between Husserl's transcendental phenomenology and Heidegger's hermeneutic phenomenology, becomes very obscure. The aim of this work is to dispel some of that obscurity.

The idea of studying the relation between these thinkers is certainly not new. Many scholars have devoted a great deal of research to the problem. Ernst Tugendhat, for example, focuses upon the concept of truth as the guiding clue in his comparison, presented in *Der Wahrheitsbegriff bei Husserl und Heidegger*.[3] Other thinkers such as Eugen Fink, Rudolf Boehm, Emmanuel Levinas, Paul Ricoeur, Walter Biemal, William Richardson, Joseph Kockelmans, and Robert Sokolowski, to name just a few, have contributed to a growing appreciation of the nature and importance of reawakening a "dialogue" between Husserl and Heidegger. The interpretation presented in the following page tries to work in this vein, using these authors' insights where possible. My own contribution will be to focus the issue on the nature of the *transcendental* problematic in Husserl by examining the underlying question which fosters the transcendental turn. Can this question, for example, be seen as a way of formulating the question of the meaning of 'Being' without doing a disservice to the nature of Husserl's thought? And if so, does this not provide the possibility for a more adequate understanding of the relation between Husserl and Heidegger?

In the pages to follow it will be argued that one of the major obstacles to understanding this relation resides in confusions about the meaning of the transcendental reduction itself. Until we can understand the problem to which the transcendental reduction is a response, its significance as the central concept of Husserl's phenomenology, and hence the fundamental meaning of Husserl's phenomenology as well, remains indeterminate. Thus, the only secure interpretative foundation for comprehending the philosophical relationship between Husserl and Heidegger is a grasp of the transcendental problematic in the former.

The need for this can be made evident if we turn to certain apparent *aporiai* (impasses) which threaten our project from the outset. Heidegger claims, for example, that "phenomenology is our way of access to what is to be the theme of ontology."[4] And further, "with regard to its subject-matter, phenomenology is the science of the Being of entities—ontology."[5] Husserl's transcendental reduction, on the other hand, is often described as "the bracketing of Being." Furthermore, the emphasis that Husserl places on the fact-essence dichotomy leads to phenomenology, as an eidetic science, turning away from factual existence. If Being is understood in terms of factual, empirical reality, Husserl's phenomenology, it might be said, seems singularly nonontological. Thus, how can there be any talk of a ground of continuity between the two authors when, from the outset, their problematics seem to be antithetical?

In addition, there remains the often cited disparity between the Husserlian transcendental subjectivity, characterized as "wordless," and Heidegger's understanding of *Dasein* as Being-in-the-World. What is effected via the transcendental reduction is a transcendence *of* the world, a purification of consciousness from all worldly or mundane elements; while Heidegger describes *Dasein* as being transcendence *toward* the world. Hence, on two essential fronts Husserl's transcendental phenomenology shows itself as apparently in complete opposition to the central problematic of the hermeneutic phenomenology of *Being and Time*. A bracketing of Being seems to be just another variant of the forgottenness of Being which Heidegger claims is symptomatic of the Western metaphysical tradition. And, moreover, the idea of a worldless subjectivity is precisely the notion that *Being and Time*, through the claim that *Dasein is* Being-in-the-World, attempts to eradicate. From such a perspective, the transcendental reduction appears as the fundamental ground of difference between Husserl and Heidegger, a difference which is indeed irreduceable.

This manner of posing the problem, however, presupposes a variety of points, not the least of which is a definite understanding of the transcendental reduction. The apparent turn away from ontology through the transcendental reduction is often attributed to epistemological motives. It might be said, for example, the Husserl's quest for an apodictic beginning point, for an indubitable epistemic foundation, results in a surrender of the ontological problematic. The elimination of contingency seemingly necessitates the exclusion of the problem of Being. This quest for apodicticity, for an evidential moment which excludes, a priori, even the possibility of doubt, is part of the Cartesianism of Husserl. The scientific ideal of an absolute beginning point is thus seen as the basic problem which occasions the transcendental reduction.

But does such a view of Husserl's Cartesianism really do justice to the nature of the transcendental reduction? And, accordingly, is this Cartesianism the focal point for a Heideggerian critique of transcendental phenomenology? Is the absolute at which the transcendental turn is directed, in the final analysis, an epistemological absolute? Or is the absolute which Husserl attempts to establish of another nature? In any event, the allegedly absolute character of transcendental subjectivity must be made a theme of investigation, so that an authentic contrast with the Heideggerian position will be possible.

How can we bring this absolute into vision so as to see it correctly in relation to what we shall call the Cartesian ideal of apodicticity? In *Husserl und Kant,*[6] Iso Kern enumerates three different ways to the transcendental reduction in Husserl: the way through ontology, the way through intentional psychology, and the way through Cartesianism. The last is the predominant manner of introducing phenomenology in *The Idea of Phenomenology, Ideas I,* and the *Cartesian Meditations.* Hence, these are the most Cartesian of Husserl's works, and so provide the best material for grasping the extent to which the ideal of apodicticity functions as the guiding *telos* behind the transcendental turn.

Kern mentions four different characteristics of the Cartesian way to the reduction:

1. The idea of philosophy as an absolutely grounded science, rooted in an absolute, indubitable (clear and distinct) evidence
2. A universal critique of our knowledge of the transcendent world, disclosing it as nonapodictic *in principle*
3. The discovery of the *cogito* as an absolute beginning point
4. The explication of the intentionality of the *cogito,* and on this basis, the reemergence of the world as *cogitatum.*[7]

We shall attempt, in the following pages, to study the Cartesian way with an eye to these structures in order to see the extent to which the unfolding of the transcendental problematic, in its deepest meaning, coincides with these ideas. In particular, *Ideas I* and the *Cartesian Meditations,* as the more developed and more influential Husserlian texts, will be explicated in detail.

Thus, the first two chapters deal with textual analyses of *Ideas I* and the *Cartesian Meditations* respectively, while Chapter 3 attempts a unified interpretation of the transcendental reduction on the basis of these analyses. With a clearer understanding of the transcendental reduction, Chapter 4 then turns to a comparison of transcendental subjectivity and Being-in-the-World.

In addition to summarizing, the final chapter shows some of the consequences of the hermeneutic beginning point (or circle) for the nature of philosophical questioning. The sections dealing with Husserl are more detailed and extensive than those on Heidegger, but this is dictated by the belief that only a careful study of the relevant Husserlian texts can remove the fatal misconceptions that foster artificial comparisons, and ultimately cover over completely the genuine philosophical matters of importance.

1
Absolute Consciousness in
Ideas I

ONE OF THE MOST controversial claims advanced by Husserl in Volume I of the *Ideas* is that consciousness is a realm of absolute being. Philosophical absolutes of any sort should always be treated cautiously. Oftentimes the appearance of such absolutes testifies more to a certain myopia on the part of their advocates than to the discovery of genuine first principles. It is often said, and perhaps with some justification, that this is true of Husserl's thought as well. An even more serious challenge, however, is posed by the view that not only is the manner in which Husserl moves to an absolute deficient, but also that the very ideal of a philosophical absolute as found in Husserl's phenomenology is little more than a relic of a kind of historical naïveté.[1]

In the pages to follow, judgment on this issue will be reserved until adequate interpretive analyses of the relevant texts have been developed. While a philosophical commitment to truth prescribes that we be wary of absolute claims, such a commitment likewise demands that the nature of the absolute in question, and the grounds advanced for it, be given a full hearing. Hence, one of the central concerns of this work will be with the nature, function, and significance of the allegedly absolute character of consciousness in Husserlian phenomenology.

First, we shall try to see the way in which this absolute emerges in *Ideas I*, reserving the development in the *Cartesian Meditations* for the next chapter. The manner in which this theme shall be approached initially will be via a contrast between the philosphical and non-philosophical attitudes, and the nature of the transition from the latter to the former. This mode of access to the problematic finds its legitimation in the fact that Husserl conceives of the domain of the absolute as the subject matter for philosphical thought. The nature of philosophical thinking takes shape in light of that about which it thinks. The same is true for nonphilosophical thinking. Thus, we begin with the posing of the problem in terms of the movement from the nonphilosophical to the philosophical.

THE PREPHILOSOPHICAL AND PHILOSOPHICAL ATTITUDES

Husserl's claim that consciousness is a realm of absolute being is the product of a lengthy meditation reflexively directed upon capturing the essence of consciousness in itself. The point of departure for this inquiry is a description of the experiential content of ordinary human life and of the presuppositions which delimit the significance of this life activity.[2] Thus, Husserl's aim, in the true spirit of phenomenology, is to avoid all conceptually bound and constructed beginnings via a descriptive return to those most general characteristics of our predominant form of experience.

Husserl begins the second section of *Ideas I*, a section intended as a preliminary introduction to the fundamental phenomenological outlook, with a brief characterization of the prephilosophical life. In so doing, Husserl is concerned with uncovering something in that life which can serve as an impetus for philosophical activity. In other words, the seeds of the transition from the prephilosophical to the philosophical must be contained in the former. Despite the widening abyss (*chorismos*) between the two in the subsequent development of the philosophical position, the possibility of such a turn must somehow be grasped within the natural life of human activity. In Plato's "myth of the cave," for example, we are never told explicitly the motive behind the first awakenings of the prisoner to the possibility of another realm beyond that of the images. It is only in the discussions of desire (*eros*) in other dialogues, as well as in the erotic tendencies exhibited by Glaucon in the *Republic* itself, for example, that we find the grounds for the transcendence of the entire realm of opinion (*doxa*). The suggestion is clear: that somehow the structure of human experience itself (*eros*), in the recognition of *doxa* as *doxa*, allows for a kind of philosophical transcendence. For in Plato, as in ancient philosophy in general, human life begins in *doxa*, and if philosophy is to be possible, therein must lie its origins.

Thus, as far as *Ideas I* is concerned, we can see that Husserl does not begin with an abstract scientific norm as the ground for philosophical reflection. There is no appeal to a historical, philosophical *telos*, nor do we begin with cognition as a developed epistemological problem.³ Rather, Husserl starts with a description of the presence of man in the world, and the presence of the world for man. His aim is to portray the most immediate way in which this encounter between man and world exhibits itself. The presence of the world of *doxa* is not exclusively one of a totality of objects to be known by a cognizing subject: "This world is not there for me as a mere world of facts and affairs, but with the same immediacy, as a world of values, a world of goods, a practical world."⁴ The question that needs to be asked bears upon the way in which this lived world not only generates sciences in the natural sense, as articulations of the laws governing the regularity of that which is given in ordinary experience (*doxa*), but also how it brings to birth philosophical reflection, and thereby delimits its nature.

A possible objection arises here, however; namely, that such a search for the ground of continuity between the naive and transcendental perspectives in Husserlian philosophy is fundamentally misdirected. Eugen Fink, for example, claims in an article authoritatively sanctioned by Husserl that from a natural or prephenomenological (prephilosophical) perspective, the transcendental turn is completely unmotivated.⁵ On the one hand it is this unmotivated character of the transcendental reduction which nonphenomenologists (neo-Kantians in particular) find so vexing.⁶ "The reduction becomes knowable only with the transcending of the world."⁷ The entire philosophical problematic generates itself anew at the transcendental level. At the same time, Fink notes, it is precisely the attempt to find motivations for transcendental phenomenology at the natural level that undermines the genuine transcendental meaning of Husserl's philosophy. For this reason, all initial presentations of the reduction and its relation to the natural attitude are inherently false: both are themselves transcendental concepts which presuppose the effective performance of the reduction.

Yet this description of the situation governing the relationship between the prephilosophical and the philosophical in no way obviates the legitimacy of the preceding reflections. The entire spiritual force of Husserl's phenomenology lies in the demand that one *see* what is meant. Phenomenological speech is descriptive speech, whose purpose is not to generate an accurate image of the original, but rather to make the original itself evident to clear intuition. The truth or falsity of this speech lies in its ability to render the phenomena intuitable in themselves. It must be recognized that all of Husserl's major works published in his lifetime are *introductions* to phenomenology. They do not present a complete system of results as the product of phenomenological reflection, but rather beckon the reader to engage actively, along with the author, in the philosophical activity. If we return to the example of Plato's "myth of the cave," we can say that Husserl's works aim at showing the reader the way up to the sunlight, and not simply at describing the world of reality so that the cave dwellers might evaluate such results in light of the norms governing doxic life.[8]

Thus, when Fink claims that all initial accounts of the phenomenological reduction are necessarily false, he is correct to the extent that the meaning of the reduction, and correlatively of transcendental subjectivity, has not yet been brought to full intuition. Inappropriate interpretive horizons structure our initial intuitions so as to cover over the full significance of the phenomena. But this cannot mean that these accounts fail to "re-present" the reality under discussion, for the phenomenological conception of truth is not a representational one. Phenomenologically speaking, these accounts are false if they "cover up" the phenomena which they intend to disclose. The adequacy of certain ways to the reduction, for example, and the accuracy of certain formulations of what is being pointed to, are indeed legitimate questions of debate. But to claim that the falsity involved in all initial characterizations of phenomenological consciousness is something other than this, or something other than the incompleteness of the yet-to-be-fulfilled intuitions is to misunderstand the intuitional character of Husserl's thought from the ground up.

We can see, therefore, that the task of uncovering the impetus for the philosophical in the prephilosophical life is not eliminated by the nonworldly nature of transcendental consciousness. From the standpoint of transcendental philosophy, the mundane or naive world of experience can be fully understood only when traced to its origins in transcendental subjectivity. Any form of inquiry or investigation, reflexive or otherwise, which remains strictly within the realm of the doxic, is doomed to an incompleteness in principle. For the natural attitude works with presuppositions (regarding Being, existence, transcendence, truth, possibility, actuality, relations, etc.) which always remain unclarified. Yet transcendental consciousness, in turn, despite its essential lack of dependence upon the world, is what it is only in its interrelationship with the world.[9] The ideal possibility of a transcendental subjectivity for which there is no world, whose constitutive activities lack the regularity of synthesis according to a priori rules, need not immediately concern us here. Perhaps for such a consciousness there would be no world, no natural attitude, no prephilosophical position, and hence no philosophy as a distinctive striving for a holistic comprehension of that life. Our concern is to come to terms with the motives for the philosophical enterprise, and the ideal possibility uncovered in eidetic intuition of a consciousness for which neither philosophy nor natural life has significance is vacuous.

The purpose of these considerations is the establishment of the fact that there are determinate and concrete ties in Husserl's phenomenology between the natural and the philosophical attitudes. Moreover, it is only through an analysis of these connections that the deepest motives, the original philosophical *telos*, underlying Husserl's transcendental turn can be unveiled. At the same time, we wish to preserve the distinction, in all its fullness, between these two attitudes. Our question bears upon the way in which the prephilosophical structures the philosophical problematic, while simultaneously is completely transcended by the latter. Husserl insists that as long as we remain bound to the natural attitude and to the presupposed criteria for intelligibility which are functional therein, we are barred from grasping the distinctive meaning of any transcendental concept.

If we take, for example, what is entailed in the notion of constitutive phenomenology, and the attempt to think of the relation between the self and its objects without performing the transcendental reduction, then the transcendental concept of constitution is completely unintelligible. We might insist, for example, that the relation between self and world, or between self and objects in the world, is either creative, receptive, or some combination of these two.[10] Constitution must lie somewhere under these headings. But Husserl's claim is precisely that constitution, as the genesis of meaning, cannot be grasped in terms of these worldly concepts. Such concepts are mundane and presuppose a ground of relation as well as an ontological concept of *relata*. The meaning of this concept (transcendental or not) becomes determinate when one sees the phenomena to which it refers.[11] In the case of constitution the phenomenon is a transcendental one, a transcendental experience which is to be seen nowhere "in the world." From a worldly or doxic perspective, it is completely unintelligible.

If the world of experience is the whole, the ultimate horizon of meaning, then such a transcendental concept must be as opaque and senseless as would be an account of the realm of genuine sunlight

intuition replaces experience ₄ (Erfahrung)

to the Plantonic cave dwellers. No descriptive accounts aimed at *representation* will be of any value until one can be brought to see. This is why intuition must replace experience (*Erfahrung*) as the ultimate court of appeal, if the realm of *doxa* is to be disclosed as *doxa*, and not presupposed as the whole.[12]

This example of the concept of constitution was drawn upon to stress the radical split between the transcendental and the nontranscendental in Husserlian phenomenology. Husserl's phenomenology necessarily becomes constitutive phenomenology once the transcendental turn is effected. Thus, what emerges as the genuine philosophical problematic, namely problems of constitution, are meaningless from the prephilosophical perspective. Not only does the positive work of solving these problems via transcendental reflection and analysis remain unintelligible from the natural standpoint, but more radically, from such a perspective these problems don't even exist. Transcendental phenomenology not only generates unintelligible solutions, but creates its own problems as well: "therefore, phenomenology's basic problem does not even exist before the performance of the reduction."[13] And furthermore, "there is no problem already given within the world which can serve to occasion our setting phenomenology into practice."[14]

But at the same time, it must be recognized that constitutive phenomenology, both with respect to its problems and its solutions, is not really generated *ex nihilo*. There may be a total transmutation of an original problematic when it is raised to the transcendental level, yet the original problem still persists, even if only in a "determinately negated" fashion. In other words, the interrelation and inner dynamic between the prephilosophical and philosophical states of mind bear a resemblance to the kind of Hegelian dialectic found in the *Phenomenology of Spirit* whereby an earlier stage of consciousness is preserved in a determinately negated form in the *Experience* of a higher level.[15] The world for natural consciousness and the world seen by transcendental consciousness as the noematic correlate of constitutive intentionality is the identically same world. The positive doctrine of constitution is an immediate response to a transcendental problem, and the latter is a reformulation of a pretranscendental world problem which retains an identity within difference with the original.

Archimedean point —

THE PROBLEM OF THE REDUCTION

But what is the pretranscendental (pre-philosophical) world problem which occasions the radical reflexivity of phenomenology? Is it a problem of knowledge in the sense of a quest for epistemic certitude? Is the absolute sought by Husserl an epistemological one which would function as a kind of Archimedean point? Is the beginning question of philosophy directed toward that which is first in the order of knowledge? The question of knowledge, posed in terms of certitude or indubitability, can arise within a world-immanent framework and hence readily suggests itself as the motive underlying the turn to the subject in Husserl's thought.[16] As such, it would provide a ground of continuity between the transcendental and pretranscendental, a question raised at one level finding its answer at another. This line of interpretation elevates apodictic certitude to the status of the final cause underlying the Husserlian project.

A second possibility, however, is that the guiding concern animating the development of transcendental phenomenology is more oriented toward the question of the Being of the world. This would suggest that an ontological problematic is at the root of Husserl's turn to subjectivity. Or are these two problems identical? Is the ancient dictum of Parmenides, that "thought and Being are the same," applicable in this context as well? And if not, just how are we to see the relationship between the epistemologically directed quest for apodicticity and the ontological problem of the Being of the world? This is a complex and difficult question, and if any light can be shed on it, it will only come at the end of our analyses. For now, let us look to the way in which Husserl introduces the motives for the transcendental turn in *Ideas I*.

A description of prephilosophical life uncovers the general thesis of the "Being out there" of the natural world.

> I find continually present and standing over against me the one spatio-temporal fact world (*Wirklichkeit*), to which I myself belong. . . . This fact world . . . I find to be "out there," and also take it just as it gives itself to me as something that exists out there.[17]

From a scientific standpoint which remains within the context of this given world, there occurs a certain *natural* identification of various ontological conceptions. That is to say, the concepts true Being, real Being, i.e., real empirical Being, and—since all that is real comes to self-concentration in the form of a cosmic unity (*zur Einheit der Welt*)—"Being in the world" are meanings that coincide.[18]

The latter formulation is a reflective one based upon the pregiven data found in the former. It is a kind of fledgling philosophical realism, a realism which, as presupposed, supplies the backdrop for all particular and determinate forms of human interaction and expression.

Thus, what Husserl claims to be at the core of ordinary experiential life is the unrelenting Being as presence of the world. From a modern theoretical position, one which is explicitly linked with the above-mentioned realism, "the world is the totality of objects that can be known through experience."[19] But from a pretheoretical position, one which forms the point of departure for the introduction to phenomenology in *Ideas I*, the world is simply that which, "prior to any thinking, bears in its totality and in all its articulated sections the character 'present,' 'out there.'"[20] The three characteristics, then, of the world as lived prephilosophically are: (a) its presence, that it is *vorhanden*; (b) that it is "out there" (*da*), that it has *Dasein*; and (c) that these attributes are prior to any judgmental act; that the world is already present, out there, independently of our thinking it.

It is within this context that Husserl first introduces the important phenomenological concept of horizons. The co-presence of self and world which lies at the basis of the natural attitude cannot be thought wholly in terms of a spatial proximity between two discrete entities. Such an analogy is one dimensional. While there may always be a focal point for our experiential life in terms of a particular and determinate object, such determinancy always takes shape against a background of indeterminacy.[21] Thus there are two components through which the prephilosophical world emerges, as a co-presence of determinancy and indeterminacy. Accompanying any determinate act is an indeterminate horizon, which, in natural experience (in contrast, for example, to mathematics) is of a spatio-temporal nature. It is the interplay of these two forms of presence and absence which constitutes the dynamic of human life.

The way in which the world announces itself, the how of its *Dasein* and *Vorhandenheit*, its presence "out there," takes place at three different levels. The worldly character of the world which Husserl is describing as the primal phenomenon of prephilosophical life possesses an inner complexity which must be understood if any meaningful transition to a philosophical level is to be effected. At the first level we have the pregiven existence of particular determinate realities. These may be other people, aesthetic objects, particular moral dilemmas or theoretical problems, and so forth. Husserl draws upon perception as an exemplary form of intuitive presencing in accounting for this level. Accompanying any such particular instances are the immediate coperceived or coapprehended surroundings. Acts of meaning not only seize the particular, but simultaneously illuminate a field of particulars. Just as in greeting a friend in a crowd I select him over a multitude of other persons who are also present, or in reflecting upon a particular moral decision I coapprehend the immediate antecedent and consequent events, a selected particular gains its determinations in a field of particulars.

At a third level, however, is the infinite indeterminacy of that "misty horizon" which Husserl calls "the form of the world as world."[22] All of these levels are contained in each lived moment and bestow upon our prereflective, prephilosophical life a specific tone and character. But this last level, as *world form*, is the continual presupposition of the natural attitude. Within it all particular affirmations and negations take place. Through the movement of experiential life we not only change our minds about *what* things are, but also about the very fact *that* they are at all. This happens not only at the level of particulars, for we can also deny the existence of an entire region of Being. In combatting a dualism, for example, we may deny that mind or spirit *is*; all that is, is body qua matter in motion. Such a "scientific" position leaves untouched the thesis of the world, merely reinterpreting the phenomena that present themselves against its background.

The thesis of the world, then, is not a product of any cognitive or judgmental act, nor the result of a multiplicity of such acts. We can bring the thesis of the world to explicit judgmental form, but we do so only upon the basis of a prior experience of this phenomenon. But "experience" again, is used only analogically here, for experience (or intuition in general) gives us only particulars, or multiplicities of such particulars. Of course these particulars need not be facts, as spatio-temporally individuated, but can be essences as well. Yet nowhere do we find, as the correlate of any particular act, nor as the product of a synthesis of such acts, the *world form* as infinite horizon. It is always already there, as the ultimate presupposition for human activity. This is why when Husserl does introduce the *epoche* he insists that it cannot be accomplished through the bracketing of particulars, even if that were to be carried out ad infinitum. It must be done in one stroke, through which the *holistic* nature of the "world-presupposition" is put out of play.

We can say, therefore, that what has emerged at the core of natural human life is a certain thesis concerning the Being of the world. Here Being is understood in the sense of *Dasein*, though obviously not in the Heideggerian sense. What is at issue is the most primitive differentiation between self and nonself: that I am, and that others (both things and persons) are, and that we share a common world. All higher forms of cultural interaction and achievement, all forms of community, presuppose the legitimacy of this initial distinction. Husserl sees this at the vital center of experiential life. Thus, all consciousness is essentially intentional.

But how are we to understand the introduction of the phenomenological *epoche* and reductions through such reflections? Even if we grant Husserl this moment of pure description, what motives emerge therein for transcendental philosophy? Why alter, or attempt to alter, this standpoint which affirms the "being out there" of particular entities against the background of a *world form*? Sections 31 and 32 of *Ideas I* are directed toward the establishment of the possibility, on grounds of principle, of altering this thesis. But why? With respect to motives, none seem immediately forthcoming. Husserl claims it to be a possibility which lies within our perfect freedom. But why this possibility rather than others for which we are free? Does this apparent lack of motivation affirm Fink's previously mentioned thesis? Or are the motives essentially epistemological? Is this not really the problem of epistemic transcendence, of knowledge and certitude? Does not Husserl directly proceed to establish a sphere of beings which is absolute and indubitable? And thus, does not the deepest motive lie in the demand for apodicticity, a demand intrinsic to the idea of "rigorous science"? Let us simply allow Husserl to answer. With respect to the being and presence of the world and the alteration of the thesis which presupposes and affirms it, he says:

> A procedure of this sort, possible at any time, is for instance, the attempt to doubt everything which Descartes, with an entirely different end in view, with the purpose of setting up an absolutely indubitable sphere of Being, undertook to carry through.[23]

Thus, whatever the motives are for the phenomenological *epoche*, they clearly are *not* epistemological in the Cartesian sense. Such a quest for apodicticity is explicitly rejected by Husserl. We must be cautious not to confuse a possible product of the *epoche*, a concept of apodicticity, with its philosophical *telos*. Correlatively, we must not presuppose that either an exhaustive or original account of its meaning is accomplished when we focus upon the indubitability of the *cogito*.

The suggestion that I would put forth in contrast to these previously mentioned interpretations of the *epoche*, is that the deepest motives underlying this philosophical turn are ontological in nature. In general, Husserl's use of *ontology* is limited to those discussions of regional eidetics as material ontologies, as well as formal ontology.[24] These are eidetic disciplines concerned with the delimitation of the Being of objects, with regard to particular types of objectivity, and objectivity in general, respectively. They seek to discover a priori truths concerning the essential "whatness" of objects. Such eidetic sciences, however, presuppose the "thatness" (*Dasein*) of the objectivities in question. But it is precisely the positing of this "being there already" that forms the essence of the natural attitude. And neither material nor formal ontologies come to terms with this aspect of the ontological problematic. This is why transcendental consciousness proves to be "the original category of Being."[25] A doctrine of categories (material or formal) is directed toward the essential "whatness" of objects. But it presupposes the more primordial concept of transcendental Being, in and through which transcendent beings come to be as beings.

It should be noted, however, that there is a certain lack of continuity in the development of the fundamental phenomenological outlook in Part II of *Ideas I*. First we find descriptions of prephilosophical life, focusing upon certain theses concerning the Being of the world. Next comes the suggestion that this can be altered. To live in the continual mode of affirmation regarding the Being of particular beings is obviously not exhaustive. But what Husserl is claiming is that beyond such particular suspensions, or a multiplicity of such suspensions, lies the possibility of a wholistic suspension of the thesis of the *world form* itself. The only possible motivation for such a move that retains the ontological sense of the problematic which animated it is a radical "science of Being."[26] We must render the origins of the general thesis transparent in order to comprehend its meaning. But upon what basis is a science of Being in this sense to be erected? In asking, "What can remain over when the whole world is bracketed?"[27] Husserl is posing the question of the context within which, or the standpoint from which, this philosophy is to emerge.

It is obvious that, like every other intelligible problem, the transcendental problem derives the means of its solution from an existence stratum which it presupposes and sets beyond the research of its inquiry.[28]

The difficulty lies in finding such an "existence-stratum" which is not a product of the affirmation of the Being of the world. The possibility of presupposing its existence, insofar as the ideal of a full philosophical account is concerned, is excluded in the case of phenomenological reflection, for it is just this seemingly universal existential presupposition which the *epoche* wishes to make thematic. What is so curious is that in securing this realm, Husserl initiates a series of psychological reflections. The connection between psychology and a science of Being can only be intimated here insofar as we know that establishing a realm of Being which does not presuppose the affirmation of worldly Being is the governing idea behind these thoughts.

If we are to understand the way in which the science of psychology and a science of Being are interrelated, we must look carefully at the movement of thought whereby psychology is transcended. And this movement is none other than that from the prephilosophical to the philosophical.

THE WAY TO THE REDUCTION IN *IDEAS I*

With the beginning of the second chapter of Part II, Husserl initiates the transition from the empty or formal possibility of a universal *epoche,* to the question of its meaning qua serviceability. What possible function could this alteration of perspectives serve? More pressing than the specific function, however, is the possibility of any function whatsoever. That is to say, if the universal *epoche* carried out with respect to the existence of what is, is truly universal, no content would remain which might be made a theme of reflection. If the source of all existence, with respect to its meaning, lies in the thesis of the natural attitude which affirms the being out there of the world, and ultimately of all transcendent entities, then all Being, all existence, falls within the scope of such an *epoche.* Nothing would thereby remain after this abstention but silence.

How could the *epoche* be limited so as to leave a residum of some sort?[29] The possibility of such a limitation, which would simultaneously preserve the true nature of the *epoche*, could only emerge insofar as an existence-stratum, or region of beings, were discovered which does not rely upon the thesis of the natural attitude for the sense of its existence. But this involves denying the wholistic claim inherent in the natural attitude. The concepts "true Being," "real Being," and "Being in the world" can no longer coincide.[30] What Husserl hopes to show is that consciousness, when considered in its purity, is not a being in the world. This is the "yet to be defined" distinctive characteristic of the new region whose discovery marks the genuine *telos* of phenomenological reflection.

Husserl begins his line of thought, then, with a phenomenological psychology, one which proceeds on the basis of the natural attitude. We abstract from the realm of physical phenomena to the psychical, considering lived experiences as part of the whole which is the world. We assume the distinction between nature and consciousness, two parts whose sum equals all that is real. In Sections 35 through 38 certain essential characteristics of lived experience (*Erlebnisse*) are discovered, characteristics which will reinforce this distinction between nature and consciousness. First, it belongs to the essence of consciousness that it be differentiated into the modes of actuality and inactuality; that is, "the stream of experience can never consist wholly of focal actualities."[31] Second, all consciousness is intentional.[32] Third, all consciousness is characterized by a directedness of the ego towards an object, thus moving away from the non-egological position of the *Logical Investigations*. This intentional directedness which persists throughout the modal alterations between actuality and inactuality has the structure of *ego-cogito-cogitatum*. And fourth, to the essence of each *cogitatio* "belongs in principle the possibility of a 'reflexive' directing of the mental glance toward itself naturally in the form of a new *cogitatio* and by way of a simple apprehension."[33]

It is on the basis of these eidetic descriptions that we come to learn what consciousness is in itself. This kind of eidetic psychology constitutes a regional ontology. And it is only one of a multiplicity of such ontologies which are necessary if we are to clarify the essential differences between various kinds of "beings in the world." In this regard, Husserl can be seen as implementing Brentano's demand for a scientific distinction between the psychical and physical, now with the aid of the method of essential intuition. As a particular material ontology, eidetic psychology has a formal ontology standing above it, though not in the form of a higher genus.[34] But this does not immediately imply that these two types of ontology exhaust the entire Being problematic. Have we said everything that can be said about the objectivity of the object, or about the subjectivity of the subject, when they have been considered both in terms of their formal and material a priori structures?

It should noted that beginning with Section 39 of *Ideas I*, the investigation takes a fundamentally new direction. A certain plateau has been reached such that Husserl now introduces reflections on the *existence* of those particulars which are instances of the essences thus far disclosed. If there are to be any *real* particulars which instantiate these eidetic characteristics, it seems that they must belong as "real events to the natural world."[35] This claim is not derived from the preceding psychological reflections, but rather is presupposed by them, just insofar as they are psychological, that is, viewed within the presupposed world form.

Section 38 must be taken as a transitional point. Not only is the essential property of reflexivity introduced as a fourth eidetic character of consciousness seen psychologically, but also the "how" of the presence of consciousness to itself in such reflection is mentioned. Husserl draws the distinction between immanent and transcendent perceptions, claiming that for the former, "their intentional objects, when these exist (*existieren*) at all, belong to the same stream of experience as themselves."[36] Here we have a consideration of the existence of conscious acts introduced within a purely eidetic context. This transition from essence to existence, however, should not be taken as a logical implication, such as in the ontological argument of Anselm, for Husserl as noted above, specifically says, "when they exist at all." *If* the objects of immanent acts exist, then they must belong to the same stream as those acts. This is intended as an essential truth which, like all essential truths, does not establish the fact of existence. Yet it is an essential truth about existence, or more particularly, about the locus of existence.

The significance of this onset cannot be underestimated for the proper understanding of Husserl's claims concerning the absolute nature of consciousness. None of the other eidetic truths related to the existence of consciousness in any fashion. To assert that consciousness is modally differentiated in terms of possibility and actuality, that it is intentional, that it is directed from an ego pole (egological) toward an object (*cogitatum*) pole—all claim what consciousness is, regardless of its existence. The existence aspect is simply presupposed as a psychical, physical, or psycho-physical event in the real world. But with the claim concerning the locus of the existence of the objects of immanently directed acts, a new dimension is introduced, one which is to provide the possibility for a more complete ontological characterization of the phenomena in question.

Within this stream there is an essentially unmediated unity between act and object. Such essential unity is lacking in transcendently directed acts.

> The perception of a thing not only does not contain in itself, in its *reellen* constitution, the thing itself, it is also without any essential unity with it, its existence naturally presupposed.[37]

Here again we return to the presuppositional nature of existence which is the theme of the thesis of the natural attitude. It is at this point in the text that the thesis of the natural attitude, phenomenological psychology, and transcendental phenomenology converge. The theme is existence, and with existence we are brought to the verge of the transcendental-philosophical domain.

In emphasizing the theme of existence in this fashion, we must continually keep in mind that the investigations are still eidetic in nature. Essential analyses can never establish the *fact* of existence. Judgments about the fact of existence, whether or not a certain thing or reality *is*, must take place under the guidance of "existence-giving" modes of intuition. Not all "object-giving" modes of intuition present consciousness with allegedly factual objects or states of affairs. Eidetic intuition, for example, gives "irreal" or ideal essences. But while such intuition cannot render evidence for the fact of existence, Husserl claims that it nonetheless can disclose the meaning of the existence of different types of objectivity. In other words, if I want to know whether a certain thing exists or not, I will turn to empirical experience. Eidetic intuition is not intended to replace a defective form of access to reality, as if only a separate faculty of reason gives us truths about the world. But if I want to know what I mean when I claim, on the basis of that empirical experience, that a certain thing exists, then I must turn to an eidetic investigation, and ultimately, Husserl will contend, an eidetic investigatin of transcendental subjectivity.

It should not be surprising, therefore, that in Section 39 and following, a new line of inquiry is undertaken. Up to this point

Husserl's concern has been with the essence of consciousness; with those characteristics which it necessarily possesses just insofar as it is consciousness. As an a priori science concerned with a concrete region, and not with the pure form of objectivity in general, this eidetic psychology is a material ontology. As such, however, it is laden with "existential" presuppositions. And this is precisely what Husserl points out at the beginning of Section 39.

> Our inquiries were eidetic; but the individaul instances of the essences we have referred to as experience, stream of experience, "consciousness" in all its senses, belonged as real events to the natural world.[38]

Working within the confines of a psychological *epoche*, physical nature and its relation to the psychically immanent need not be made a theme, any more than the physicist must clarify the psychological dimension to his *knowledge of* nature. But even in the absence of specific thematization, the presuppositions of the natural attitude regarding the existence of conscious experiences still function as an interpretive horizon whereby acts are grasped *as* real, spatio-temporal events within the one, universal, causally interrelated nexus of the world.

Husserl's task in the sections to follow is to render explicit that *as*, to trace it to its "ultimate source,"[39] to examine its credentials and legitimacy insofar as its claims are wholistic in nature. In other words, from the pretranscendental perspective,

> consciousness and thinghood form a connected whole, connected within the particular psychological unities which we call *animalia*, and in the last resort within the real unity of the world as a whole.[40]

The question which is asked bears upon the unity of the whole; that is,

> can the unity of a whole be other than made one through the essential proper nature of its parts, which must therefore have some community of essence instead of fundamental heterogeneity?[41]

The way in which this inquiry is pursued is in terms of the existence of consciousness and the existence of thinghood; the latter chosen only as an exemplary form of all transcendent objectivity.

If the philosophical (transcendental) level is to be attained, the existence problematic itself must be introduced. What it means for a being to be can no longer be straightforwardly posited by the general thesis of the natural, prephilosophical life. From Husserl's perspective, all traditional insoluble dilemmas of philosophy (what the Greeks called *aporiai*, as well as all illegitimate forms of philosophical realism and idealism, are nourished by the thesis of the natural attitude concerning the existence of the *ontos on*, the "really real." Husserl will attemmpt to clarify the sense of the existence of beings by returning to that source from which their existential meaning is determined. And this return to origins is a return to *modes of givenness*, whereby the very event of self-presencing (*leibhatigen*) takes place. As Levinas correctly points out, Husserl's project is to locate existence in the presence of things to conscious life, and not in a hypothetical mute opposition.[42]

But the temptation again arises to interpret the meaning of these reflections as basically epistemological. To talk about "modes of givenness" is to talk about the "for us"; what is at issue is a characteristic of human knowledge and not of the things themselves. A being's mode of givenness discloses the way in which that entity is given to a *human* subject, and these ways are products of our forms of knowing. But Husserl anticipates this possible line of interpretation, and devotes the entirety of Section 43 to rejecting it. What he attacks here is the well known Kantian distinction between the finite and infinite intellect. It is thus a critique of Kant himself, as well as of neo-Kantian interpretations of Husserl's own work.

Husserl's position is that reflection on the modes of givenness of different types of objects discloses something about the objects themselves, and not merely something about our finite forms of knowledge. To posit an infinite intellect for whom natural objects are not given perspectively is an absurdity, for it subverts the very meaning of the Being of the objectivity in question. If God is to know nature as nature, then he knows it perspectively, and hence imperfectly. This imperfection is a negativity built into the very Being of nature, and as long as nature is to be nature, this characteristic of its existence must be preserved.

Thus an object discloses itself as it does, via a particular mode of givenness, according to laws of its own content. Perception, for example, of a physical object is perspectival "in accordance with the object's own meaning."[43] This existential emphasis upon modes of givenness holds for immanent objects as well. It is a product of their existential sense that they do not show themselves through a plurality of aspects, but rather as "fully" and "bodily" present to intuitive reflection. The question is not how *man* comes to know, but how *things* admit of being known. The epistemological characteristics rest upon an ontological basis. Via a consideration of modes of givenness, Husserl claims to have passed beyond a treatment of human (finite) forms of knowing (cognition) to the objectivity of the object itself. Moreover, these reflections penetrate to a level beyond that of either material or formal ontologies. This level is *existence* itself.

THE ABSOLUTE OF CONSCIOUSNESS

On the basis of these insights, Husserl proceeds to posit the absolute Being of the immanent and the merely phenomenal Being of the transcendent. There has yet to be any consideration of the dubitable and the indubitable, the adequate, apodictic, or assertoric. No such Cartesian epistemological conceptions are yet present. Furthermore, Husserl has specifically and emphatically rejected any attempt to interpret the results obtained thus far as bearing on our forms of knowledge alone. If all our *noeses* of the transcendent give us only perspectives, this is a result of the kind of existence belonging to the transcendent, and of the correlation between the noetic and noematic.

What has been brought to our attention, therefore, is one vital distinction between the meaning of the existence of the immanent and the meaning of the existence of the transcendent. In order to say that "consciousness is" and to say that "reality is," one must recognize the fundamental equivocation on the verb "to be." It cannot be claimed, then, that Husserl and Kant both deny existence to be a predicate. For the most fundamental difference in Husserl's thought, that between the transcendental and the nontranscendental, is grounded in the distinction between the sense of existence in the two. Simply because Husserl's phenomenology is eidetic, and hence does not establish the fact of existence, does not exclude it from considering the meaning of existence. As we have seen, what Husserl has established thus far is that, "It is an *essentially* valid law that *existence* in the form of a thing is never demanded as necessary by virtue of its givenness."[44] And in contrast, "*Every* immanent perception necessarily guarantees the *existence* of its object."[45] At the level of material ontologies the consideration of existence as a predicate may be superfluous, but a full philosophical account of the Being of entities must recognize the fundamental difference in the very existence of consciousness and transcendent reality.

This opposition between perspectival and non-perspectival modes of givenness, however, is only one dimension to the question of the meaning of the existence of the immanent and transcendent. Another aspect of the same issue bears upon the notions of "unperceived experience" and "unperceived reality."[46] Before we can turn our attention to this dimension of the existence of beings, however, we must clarify the sense of the absolute givenness of the immanent in reflection. In claiming that an experience is given absolutely in reflection, in accordance with its existential sense, Husserl is not saying that an experience so given is perceived in its completeness. The incompleteness or *inadequacy* which manifests itself in immanent perception, however, is "fundamentally other than that which is of the essence of transcendent perception."[47] This inadequacy has to do with the temporality of consciousness itself; that any reflection upon an act finds that act within the temporal flux of living consciousness. As such, the ideal of immediate and total givenness seems continually to elude our grasp. The "unmediated unity of a single concrete *cogitatio*,"[48] which at first seemed to be within reach, is now ruptured by the all pervading temporal flow. Husserl's response to this problem, in *Ideas I* at least, is to acknowledge it and yet simultaneously to insist that the main point established in the preceding sections still retains its validity.

There persists the essential difference between givenness *through* a multiplicity of perspectives and givenness *in* a single view which may exhibit an inner, temporal multiplicity. The distinction between modes of givenness, and hence between the meaning of existence, still retains its legitimacy. If, furthermore, Husserl's main concern in these pages were epistemological, this phenomenon of temporality would immediately present a most serious challenge to the claims for apodicticity.[49] But Husserl never discusses this problem. Instead, he insists that the essential difference between the Being of consciousness and the Being of reality still holds.

We can now turn to a second major distinction between the senses of existence for experience and reality. Husserl tells us:

It is a mark of the type of Being (*Seinsart*) peculiar to experience that perceptual insight can direct its immediate, unobstructed gaze upon every real (*wirkliche*) experience, and so enter into the life of a primordial presence. This insight operates as a "reflection," and it has this remarkable peculiarity that that which is thus apprehended through perception is, in principle, characterized as something which not only is and endures within the gaze of perception, but *already was before* this gaze was directed to it.[50]

Here Husserl is discussing that characteristic of beings which we might call their "availability for perception" (or for any other form of attention). In Section 35 Husserl pointed out that a modal form of the *cogito* as act is marginal actuality. For transcendent beings, this possibility means to be already an *object* of consciousness, in the form of an item within the horizon of possible objects. Just insofar as transcendent beings are available for perception, they have already been perceived as possible objects. This is not meant to say, of course, that such objects "are" only when a subject attends to them. Husserl's position is not that of a subjective idealism, and he need make no appeals to a divine subject to account for the subsistence of independent entities. But he does insist that the only meaning which this independence can have is that such entities are "perceived" as possible objects which, at least *in principle*, could be experienced. This type of "being there already" bears only an analogical resemblance to that which is exhibited in experiential being. For in the case of lived experiences (*Erlebnisse*), their very meaning is to be there prior to any sort of reflection. That is to say, "All experiences are conscious experiences."[51] Experience is not only "consciousness of" but it is also "consciousness of consciousness of." This original, "prereflexive" awareness, therefore, is nonobjectified. All *objects* of consciousness, as intentional correlates, are products of a synthesis of a multiplicity of perspectives. As such, they are objectively constituted. Prior to any reflective consciousness, however, we are conscious of our experiencing itself. Experiences, therefore, are not constituted in the same fashion as transcendent entities.

The presence of what is actually not perceived in the world of things . . . is essentially different from that mode of Being of which we are intrinsically sensible, the Being of our inward experiences.[52]

Conscious experiences *are*, independently of any sort of thematic reflection. They bear a meaning prior to being objectified, as an objectifying activity, upon which depends the objectivity of objects. They suffer no essential dependence upon an act of reflection for the meaning of either their actual or possible existence.

We have, therefore, uncovered two essential differences between the meaning of existence for immanent and transcendent being. Again, we are merely concerned with the meaning of the "is" when we claim "consciousness is" and "reality is." Prior to Section 38 certain predications were made of consciousness at the level of a regional ontology. The mode of existence of consciousness was assumed insofar as the general thesis of the natural attitude was affirmed and active. Sections 39 and following, however, focused upon the meaning of the existence of consciousness in and through a reflexive glance directed at the modes of givenness through which all existential sense has its origins. First we find that consciousness, in contrast to transcendent things, is not given perspectively. Furthermore, consciousness is "given" prior to any reflective act; while transcendent objects are only given as modal variants of specific acts. The object of a transcendentally directed consciousness is essentially dependent upon the act of apprehending it. The object of an immanently directed act, however, does not depend essentially upon the reflecting act; for it has a nonobjectified being which founds the possibility of reflection. In addition, both of these distinctions in manners of givenness are not the products of our finite forms of knowledge, Husserl insists, but rather are derived from the meaning of the *Being as existence* of the beings in question.

We have thus traversed a path from a regional ontology of what might be termed "psychical beings," to a consideration of the absolute existence of consciousness. The meaning of the Being of consciousness, just insofar as it is at all, turns out to be something entirely different from what was originally assumed from the natural standpoint. We can now understand why the result of the *epoche* is not universal negation, and why a residuum remains. The meaning of the existence of transcendent reality is traced to its origins as the consequence of the synthetic cohesion of a multiplicity of cognitive acts. As such, it is essentially dependent on the life of consciousness. Furthermore, these syntheses can never be complete. The possibility of nonbeing, of nonexistence, is intrinsic to the meaning of the transcendent. The Being of consciousness, however, has *essential* dependence upon neither transcendent reality (worldly beings) nor upon the thematizing act of reflection. The infamous "hypothetic annihilation of the world" of Section 49 of *Ideas I* is intended as nothing other than a clarification and justification of the former point. But it must be remembered that both of these claims are eidetic and thus are not vitiated by a *factual dependence*, a theme which might be studied by a science of facts such as physiological psychology.

Husserl now proceeds to posit the absolute Being of consciousness; a position based upon insight into the meaning of the existence of consciousness uncovered via reflection on its modes of givenness. "Immanent being is therefore without doubt absolute in this sense, that in principle *nulla 're' indiget ad existendum*."[53] Here is an allusion to the Cartesian doctrine of substance, though not in the sense of substratum (*hypokeimenon*). This "substantial" absolute refers to the essential lack of dependence of consciousness, both upon the transcendent world to which it is factually related, and upon reflective acts, which themselves are only possible on the basis of the original presence of the lived experiences. But consciousness is also absolute in a second sense, in that it is the "existential realm of absolute origins."[54] With this insight, the substantial absolute becomes a *transcendental* absolute.[55] Only upon the basis of this can phenomenology become constitutive phenomenology, for all other (transcendent) beings are *relative* to consciousness, are *related back* to consciousness.

With this, the goal of the phenomenological reduction in *Ideas I* has been attained. A new region of beings has been won. Its distinctive character, however, is that it is no region at all. Instead it is the realm of transcendental, absolute Being.

> It is the original category of Being (or as we would put it, the original region) in which all other regions of Being have their root, to which they are essentially related, on which they are therefore one and all dependent in an essential way.[56]

This "original category" (*Urkategorie*) is the pure life of meaning, whose wholistic nature is not the product of mere formalization. Instead, it has been disclosed through a rigorous adherence to the phenomena of existential modes of givenness, "to the things themselves."

Consciousness exists absolutely insofar as it is the *origin* of all other beings. This is the meaning of the Being of absolute consciousness. Husserl clearly does not intend this to be taken to mean that consciousness so conceived creates beings in an ontic sense. But Husserl does insist that the very meaning of the "thinghood" of things, both that they are and what they are, depends in an essential way upon the constitutive achievements of subjectivity. No pure "in itself" lies outside this domain. The realm of possible experience is now the realm of possible intuition, possible intelligibility. Thinking of a noumenal reality in the Kantian sense brings it within the sphere of Husserl's concept of transcendental subjectivity, for such conceptual thinking, if meaningful, is still intuitive, though there may be no empirically given object.

The possibility of discovering this transcendental domain lay dormant until the question of the meaning of existence (Being) of the fact-world (*Wirklichkeit*).[57] But this question could not present itself in a radical fashion within the natural attitude, for ordinary life always presupposes existence in a distinctive and particular sense. "To be" is to be as natural, worldly entities are and as such, to be within the universal world form.[58] The tendency of the natural, prephilosophical, and scientific consciousness toward reification is grounded in the essence of the natural attitude itself. With this type of ontological reductionism which denies existence to be a predicate insofar as it is universal and univocal, even eidetic differentiations between nature and consciousness will fail to avoid a reification of the latter. Thus, for example, the significance of Brentano's discovery that consciousness is intentional was necessarily perverted just insofar as consciousness remained a part of the world. The problem of the relation between the intentional object and reality was still posed in naturalistic terms.

It should be noted, in concluding these initial reflections, that the epistemological problematic and the accompanying concepts of dubitability and indubitability, the assertoric and the apodictic, arise only *after*, and on the basis of, the ontological reflections on modes of existence. The indubitability of the "thesis of my pure ego" is, for Husserl, a product of the mode of existence of consciousness itself, while the dubitability of the transcendent is likewise a result of the existential status of transcendent reality. Husserl views these epistemological characteristics as important consequences of the ontological reflections bearing upon the meaning of the Being of the fact-world, and of transcendental subjectivity. These epistemic concepts, the allegedly animating ideas of the "Cartesian way" to the reduction, are thus clearly subordinated in *Ideas I* to the more universal, ontological problematic.

2

Philosophical Science and the Idea of Evidence

USSERL'S LECTURES DELIVERED in Paris in 1929, and published in an expanded version under the title of the *Cartesian Meditations*, take their name, as well as their ideal, from Descartes' *Meditations on First Philosophy*. In the introduction to the *Cartesian Meditations*, Husserl praises Descartes as "France's greatest thinker," and says that his *Meditations* serve as "the prototype of philosophical reflection."[1] He goes on to insist that Descartes' work contains an eternal significance, one which he believes "might infuse our times with living forces."[2] Indeed, Husserl recognizes in the Cartesian approach to philosophy and science a force which "acted quite directly on the transformation of an already developing phenomenology into a new kind of transcendental philosophy."[3] In this vein, Husserl describes his own transcendental phenomenology as a neo-Cartesianism.

In suggesting that Descartes' philosophical reflections bear an eternal significance, Husserl is claiming that they are significant at a philosophical level. The meaning of the *Meditations* is not exhausted when articulated in terms of a particular world view. The prejudices of the age are surely at work in Descartes, both with respect to medieval metaphysics and modern mathematical science. Yet to see in this work only historically conditioned ideals is to surrender the dimension of the infinite which Husserl places at the core of Western philosophical thought.[4] The material content of the *Meditations* constitutes the particular, historical way to the ideal of science pursued by Descartes. The inadequacy of this content, however, to the ideal under which Descartes labored, necessitates the rejection of the content, but not of the ideal. For Husserl, the idea of Descartes is the ideal of all science, of true philosophy, of Western humanity itself.

What then is this ideal, pregnant with an eternal significance? Is there any fashion in which we can illuminate it, as well as the alterations in our lives demanded insofar as we place ourselves under it? The scientific ideal for Descartes is the idea of philosophy, that is, of an absolute, rational grounding for all sciences. Science, in turn, provides a rational grounding for the prescientific. Hence, the idea of philosophy is of a universal, absolute, rational grounding. Husserl's allegiance to this absolute is itself absolute. It is one of the "constants" in Husserl's conception of philosophy.[5]

For Descartes, this ideal necessitated a turn to the subject at two different levels.

> First, anyone who seriously intends to become a philosopher must "once in his life" withdraw into himself and build anew all the sciences that, up to then, he had been accepting. Philosophy—wisdom (sagesse)—is the philosopher's quite personal affair. It must arise as his wisdom, as his self-acquired knowledge tending toward universality, a knowledge for which he can answer from the beginning, and at each step, by virtue of his own absolute insights.[6]

Here we have the emergence of the autonomy and radical self-responsibility of the rational individual for all his insights, both theoretical and practical.

Cartesian philosophy is revolutionary, as is all philosophy, just insofar as every conventional authority is called into question. The ancient philosophers also placed in question all traditional forms of authority as the source of norms governing human life. One could look, for example, to Book I of the Republic, in which ancestral authority, religion, and poetry are undermined by Socrates. This clearing of the grounds in a search for grounds is a dangerous activity, for it not only supplies the possibility for the emergence of philosophical dialogue, but also furnishes those conditions under which sophistry can flourish. Socrates' "doubt" opens the way not only for the founding of the just city in logos, but for the appearance of Thrasymachus as well.[7]

Descartes too recognized the dangers here, and hence supplied himself with a conventional morality, one which would insure the tranquility requisite for his theoretical speculations.[8] "To begin in absolute poverty"[9] is to refuse to recognize the riches of the conventional world. The tension between philosophy and politics which manifests itself again and again throughout the history of philosophy is merely an instantiation of the tension between *episteme* and *doxa*. This opposition can show itself either within or between individuals. In either case, the activity is radically revolutionary.

It is this radical nature of philosophical reflection, expressed in Descartes' *Meditations*, which singles out the work as a paradigmatic representation of the philosophical activity. It is a life committed to complete autonomy and total self-responsibility; an existential commitment to the absolute of reason. Even when this rational striving assumes the form of communal, intersubjective labor, that to which the other leads me finds its justification "in me." All *logos*, all dialogue, has its point of authentic origin and return in intuition. To accept anything but my own insights is to surrender the autonomy of my individuality, and to renounce self-responsibility in an appeal to specific, or anonymous, external authority. If I am to accept rationally what is given to me by others, if I am to appropriate my culture rather than be conditioned by it, "I must justify it by a perfect insight on my own part. Therein consists my autonomy."[10]

This, however, constitutes only one dimension of the Cartesian turn to subjectivity. The second aspect is the discovery of "the ego as subject of his pure *cogitationes*."[11] This insight marks the birth of modern philosophy. From such a perspective, the striving of the individual for radical autonomy can be realized only via a reflection on the ego and its life. The a priori which would supply the grounds for rational insight cannot be found on the side of the object. The innate ideas of Descartes, capable of being perceived with clarity and distinctness, furnish the foundation for the rational reconstruction of the world.

It is Husserl's contention, of course, that Descartes, as well as all his successors, missed the true significance of the *ego cogito*. Descartes, on the one hand, presupposed the form which an absolute rational grounding (that is, philosophy) would take. This presupposition was of the universality of the axiomatic method of deduction. All rational grounding was modelled after mathematical rational grounding; for "no science is acquired except by mental intuition or deduction."[12] Consequently, the simple objects of intuition are immediately interpreted as axiomatic in character.

In addition to this fatal methodological presupposition, this fragmenting distortion of the notion of reason and ground, Descartes interpreted the *ego cogito* as a substance in the world. What serves as an axiom in the order of knowledge is, when seen from an ontological perspective, a part of the world. Its central status in the Cartesian philosophy is derived from its epistemological primacy, while what might be termed the ontologically first principle is reserved for the infinite substance.

The quest for the absolute beginning in Descartes, therefore, receives its determinate direction from a mathematically oriented epistemology, and from a world-immanent ontology. Hence, from Husserl's perspective, the *ego cogito*, as that beginning, is necessarily misinterpreted. Husserl's claim is that we must begin anew, in the spirit of Descartes, but more true to that spirit. We must, as it were, understand Descartes better than he understood himself.

Thus, no pregiven normative ideal of science shall be accepted. Nor can a worldly ontology be assumed as the horizon for any and all beginnings. Genuine philosophy is characterized by the genuineness of its beginnings, for "the beginning seems to be more than half the whole."[13] The central problem of philosophy is the problem of beginnings, or the return to origins which are first in themselves, the discovery of absolute rational grounds. It is in this sense that Husserl prided himself on being a beginning philosopher, for true philosophy, "first philosophy," is "a science of beginnings."[14] Thus in Husserl's reflections on his own work made in 1930, he remarks:

> The true philosophical beginning must have been irretrievably lost in beginning with presuppositions of a positive kind. Lacking as did the traditional schemes of philosophy the enthusiasm of a first beginning, they also lacked what is first and most important: a specifically philosophical groundwork acquired through original self-activity, and therewith that firmness of basis, that genuineness of root, which alone makes real philosophy possible. The author's convictions on such lines have become increasingly self-evident as his work progressed. If he has been obliged on practical grounds to lower the ideal of the philosopher to that of a downright beginner, he has at least in his old age reached for himself the complete certainty that he should thus call himself a beginner. . . . He has been able to follow up the problems that issue from the beginning, and primarily from what is first for a descriptive phenomenology, the beginning of the beginning.[15]

absolute rational grounding

What we shall attempt in this chapter, with regard to the *Cartesian Meditations*, is to catch a glimpse of this return to the beginnings, and perhaps even to the beginning of the beginning.

How is it, then, that the *Cartesian Meditations* themselves begin? The "First Meditation" has a triadic structure with regard to the problem of beginnings. It can be divided roughly in the following manner:

1. That which makes a beginning possible (Paragraphs 3–5)
2. The question of the beginning (Paragraphs 5–6)
3. The beginning of philosophy (Paragraphs 7–11)

The last problem carries over into the first two paragraphs of the "Second Meditation" in the form of some reflections on the nature of the beginning, as well as some important qualifications with respect to the genuineness of the beginning discovered in the "First Meditation."

THAT WHICH MAKES A BEGINNING POSSIBLE

Our treatment of *Ideas I* in the last chapter disclosed that in this work Husserl introduced the movement toward transcendental phenomenology in terms of an original act of freedom. The movement toward beginnings can itself begin only with the *decision* to begin. This will to begin is a will to science, a will to truth. The aim to seek an absolute rational grounding is one which can be chosen or rejected. What is presupposed, then, is the normative ideal of the general idea of science, and it is presupposed as an ethical imperative. Whether or not this ideal is capable of actualization is not something which can be presupposed. As a regulative idea governing human striving, its legitimacy is unrelated to the factual issue of whether or not it has been, or will be realized in actuality. The question is whether we *ought* to allow the regulative idea to become constitutive for our existence. Does the will to absolute rational grounding issue in a categorical, or only a hypothetical imperative? In renouncing the will to science, do we renounce only one cultural form of existence factually possible for humanity? Is the *praxis* of *theoria*,

whose aim is to elevate mankind through universal scientific reason, according to norms of truth of all forms, to transform it from the bottom up into a new humanity made capable of an absolute self-responsibility on the basis of absolute theoretical insights,[16] is this merely one among many equally valid forms of human existence?

It is beyond the scope of our considerations here to attempt a comprehensive answer to these questions from a Husserlian position. It is clear, however, that if, as Husserl says, experiential life itself is evidential,[17] then

> All life is taking a position, and all taking of position is subject to a must—that of doing justice to validity and invalidity according to alleged norms of absolute validation.[18]

The importance of the concept of evidence for Husserl's idea of man is unquestionable. From a prephenomenological point of view, Husserl sees human life in terms of position taking. In the phenomenological analyses of consciousness, this idea is articulated in terms of the identification of experience with evidence.[19] The tension within consciousness itself between presence and absence, between the intuitively apprehended and the emptily intended, provides the impetus for the movement toward the fundamental synthesis of identity constitutive of the life of consciousness. This form of synthesis, as an achievement (Leistung), is evidential.

The importance of grounds, therefore, can be seen at all levels of Husserl's thought. They function in phenomenological analyses, as well as in calls to phenomenology; they function at the predicative and prepredicative levels, at the scientific, as well as the prescientific stages. Grounding is inherent in human life itself. But this does not immediately lead us to the recognition of the necessity of rational grounds and certainly not to absolute, rational grounds. For many, sheer physical force is ground enough for legitimation. Justice is that which is in the interest of the stronger power. Or even if the desire for rational legitimation, either with regard to speech or deed, leads one to the acknowledgment of rationality (an openness to logos), why submit to the ideal of the absolute? Why not rest content with finite legitimations, with relative goods and relative truths?

Husserl, like Kant, sees reason by its very nature to be directed toward the absolute, the unconditioned, toward unity itself. Along similar lines, Plato characterizes philosophy as a tyrannical activity. This appears clearly, for example, in the political context of the Republic, with the emergence of the philosopher-king. But even in a work like the Symposium, the multiplicity of poetic speeches can no longer coexist once the Socratic speech is given. Unity and excellence (*arete*) are inseparable. To surrender the absolute of reason is to surrender reason itself. On this point, compromises are impossible.[20] All multiplicity must be seen from the perspective of a higher unity, as all deviations from law must be accountable in terms of a higher law. For just insofar as equally valid positions are copresent, the possibility of disharmony points to the need for reconciliation. In this fashion, the infinite task of reason is posed.

In the Vienna Lecture of 1935, Husserl gives an account of European culture in terms of "the historical teleology of the infinite goals of reason."[21] Human history is conceived in terms of the interplay between the finite and the infinite. It is, in the Platonic sense, a "daimonic" history. Only a humanly finite being can live toward the infinite. Only a *daimon* can say no to the apotheosis of the finite. In this lecture, as in the *Crisis*, Husserl warns that our disillusion with certain historical forms of reason must not result in the surrender to irrationalism, and hence in the end of philosophy.

> Europe's greatest danger is weariness. If we struggle against this greatest of all dangers . . . with the sort of courage that does not fear even an infinite struggle, then out of the destructive blaze of the lack of faith, the smoldering fire of despair over the West's mission for humanity, the ashes of great weariness, will rise up the phoenix of a new life-inwardness and spiritualization as the pledge of a great and distant future for man; for the spirit alone is immortal.[22]

What constitutes that which makes possible a beginning, then, is this will toward absolute autonomy and self-responsibility, chosen through an act of freedom "by anyone who seriously intends to become a philosopher."[23] This is the ideal of the scientist, the prototype of philosophy, the *telos* of Western culture. But in this form it is too vague to be able to serve meaningfully as a guiding idea. The object of our resolve can become functional only "if we immerse ourselves progressively in the characteristic intention of scientific endeavor."[24] In this way, "the constituent parts of the general final idea, genuine science, become explicated for us, though at first the differentiation is itself general."[25] It is in the context of the structural articulation of this ideal that the concept of evidence comes clearly to stand at the core of the philosophical enterprise of the *Cartesian Meditations*.

Husserl begins his clarification of the ideal of science with the notion of judicative doing and judgment.

> Judging is meaning—and, as a rule, merely supposing—that such and such exists and has such and such determinations; the judgment (what is judged) is then a merely supposed affair or complex of affairs: an affair or state of affairs, as what is meant.[26]

Judgments are differentiated into mediate and immediate, in accordance with the need for a *grounding* in other judgments. "Mediate judgments have such a sense-relatedness to other judgments that believing them 'presupposes' believing these others."[27] An immediate judgment, however, would find its ground in the givenness of the state of affairs independently of the acceptance of another judgment and its judged content.

The distinction between mediate and immediate judgments, however, in turn presupposes the striving for grounded judgments as a component of the ideal of science. The refusal to recognize this kind of relation between our judgments, as evidenced for example in the unwillingness to see the consequences of certain positions we take, testifies to irrationality on our part. To believe, for example, that modern empirical sciences can give an exhaustive account of man, and simultaneously to accept the belief in man's freedom, is to rupture the rational relation between our judgments, and to surrender the will to truth. Thus, a second facet of the ideal of science is this striving for grounded judgments, and ultimately, for immediately grounded judgments, in and through which truth and falsity can come to be tested.

The fusion of the notions of judgments and the striving for grounds gives rise to the idea of evidence; "a pre-eminent judicative meaning (*Meinen*), a judicative having of such and such itself."[28] In order to articulate this third component of the ideal of science, even in its most primitive form, Husserl has recourse to two phenomenological concepts which are crucial for all subsequent eidetic analyses: namely, fulfillment and synthesis. The movement toward evidence is a conscious conversion "inherently characterized as the fulfilling of what was merely meant, a synthesis in which what was meant coincides and agrees with what is itself given."[29]

Fulfillment presupposes the elements of absence and presence as the poles or relata which can be either fulfilled (evidence) or cancelled (negative evidence.)[30] Synthesis, in turn, presupposes unity or identity

Truth is established by evidence or intuition —
def. of truth as evidence = not mimicking
? Science

Philosophical Science and the Idea of Evidence 39

refine philosophy = search for truth = science.

as its goal. That which is emptily meant or intended and that which comes to be given in fulfillment is based upon a pregiven claim to identity between the two, an assumed identity which is the condition for the possibility of either fulfillment or cancellation.[31] Only insofar as the man about whom I make a judgment and the man whom I come to see, are meant as the identically same man, can my judgment be verified or falsified. The same is true of perception itself, which will likewise have empty and full moments.

It may be, therefore, that Ricoeur is correct in claiming that the prebeginning of the *Cartesian Meditations* is mediated by the results of the phenomenological studies of truth and evidence in the *Logical Investigations*. He claims that

ethical imperative —
BE RATIONAL!

the beginning philosophy is preceded not by a presence but (1) by a principle: the obligation to accept the idea of truth, and *will* (2) by a definition: the definition of truth by evidence.[32] *to truth = faithfulness to evidence.*

But we must note that what Ricoeur means by "definition" is a *scientific striving* definite concept of truth, rather than merely the fixed meaning of a term. Our concern in these last pages has been with that which makes a beginning possible, hence, with a prebeginning. The first element emerged as an ethical imperative: "Be rational!" This will to truth, however, necessitated a further elaboration if it was to give direction to the inquiry. In this vein, Husserl came to a precursory presentation of the idea of evidence, derived from an immersion in the scientific striving which is the will to truth. *Presupposition-less philosophy*

Husserl recognizes that we cannot begin *ex nihilo*. The ideal of a presuppositionless philosophy need not entail the complete lack of presuppositions, but rather that we accept only those presuppositions necessary for rational conduct, and recognize them as presuppositions.[33] "Everything that makes a philosophical beginning possible we must first acquire by ourselves."[34] The entire thrust of the prebeginnings is directed toward the attainment of a "first methodological principle."[35] From Husserl's perspective, the "definition" of truth as evidence is not derivative from any theory of science naively taken over in an uncritical fashion. Instead, it is *seen* in the very activity of science, of being scientific, just insofar as science is to be science. It belongs to the essence of science as a necessary and inseparable moment. The act in which we commit ourselves to being true contains the moments of presence, absence, and identity. In the langue of Platonic myth, that which we lack (absence), and yet whose possession (presence) we anticipate, is the object of *eros*. And our *eros* is directed toward possessing the same thing (identity) which we lack.

A fourth and final component of the ideal of science which Husserl discusses is the precedence of the prepredicative over predicative evidence. Judgments refer to categorial objects, which, as Sokolowski aptly describes them, are "infected with syntax."[36] A prepredicative evidence gives us the "ultimate substrate" of a judgment, that is,

> something still categorially completely unformed, a substrate which has not yet entered into a judgment and taken on a form in it, and which, just as it is self-evident and self-given, becomes for the first time a substrate of a judgment.[37]

This point will be developed in more detail in the following chapter, in the context of a "genealogy of logic,"[38] moving toward the notion of absolute *concreta*. But just as mediate judgments point back to immediate judgments, the latter are founded on the givenness of the prepredicative.

What can we say, then, about the outcome of the consideration of the prebeginnings in the *Cartesian Meditations*, in light of the articulation of the ideal presented above? Briefly formulated, it is the recognition of the identity between the Cartesian idea of science and that which governs all scientific striving, namely, the demand for evidence.[39] Truth and evidence are not limited to the judgmental realm, for the predicative rests upon a more primordial mode of givenness. That which gives objects is "experience" (intuition) in the widest possible sense, and "Evidence is, in an extremely broad sense, an *experiencing* of something that is, and is thus."[40] This leads to the formulation of the "first methodological principle," which is "our normative principle of evidence."[41]

> It is plain that I, as someone beginning philosophically, since I am striving toward the presumptive end, genuine science, must neither make nor go on accepting any judgment as scientific that I have not derived from evidence, from "experiences" in which the affairs and affair complexes in question are present to me as they themselves. Indeed, even then I must reflect at all times on the pertinent evidence; I must examine its "range" and make evident to myself how far that evidence, how far its "perfection," the actual giving of the affairs themselves, extends.[42]

Yet this is nothing other than a reformulation of the "principle of all principles" presented in *Ideas I*, namely, that

every primordial dator (*gebende*) intuition is a source of authority for knowledge, that whatever presents itself in intuition in primordial form (as it were in its bodily reality), is simply to be accepted as it gives itself out to be, though only within the limits in which it then presents itself.[43]

Husserl sees this principle as prior to all theories, for, "no theory we can conceive can mislead us in regard to it."[44] This "definition" is extracted from the very act of commitment to truth. It is in this sense that we give ourselves the prebeginning in taking up the task of being reasonable. It does not presuppose the results of the *Logical Investigations*, for they too proceed only in light of this principle.[45]

THE QUESTION OF THE BEGINNING

This leads us now to a consideration of the second aspect of the way to phenomenology in the *Cartesian Meditations*, the question of the beginning. The components of the idea of science, extracted via noematic analysis of the scientific (rational) intention, have disclosed themselves in terms of

an order of cognition, proceeding from intrinsically earlier to intrinsically later cognitions; ultimately, then, a beginning and a line of advance that are not to be chosen arbitrarily, but have their basis in the nature of the things themselves.[46]

A cognition, however, is explicable only in terms of evidence; that is, a cognition is that to which we can return, in consequence of an executed grounding. It is an identity. All identity, as has been noted, is a result of the synthetic movement from absence to presence, which is the life of experience, of evidence itself.

Husserl poses "the question of the beginning" as "the inquiry for those cognitions that are first in themselves and can support the whole storied edifice of universal knowledge."[47] What is required is a movement from that which is first for us, to that which is first in itself, "in the nature of the things themselves." For Husserl, then, the phenomenological slogan "To the things themselves" is simply an articulation of the idea of science, expressing a maxim inseparable from the decision to philosophize. It could be interpreted as the manifestation of an implicit realism in Husserl's thought only if that which is first in itself is identical with that to which a naive (or sophisticated) realism ascribes an ontological primacy. But such a primacy is something which stands in need of justification.

The question of the beginning, as posed by Husserl, is in terms of those cognitions which are first in themselves. All of his philosophy is a response to this question. Husserl's thought poses the problem of "firstness"; it is a "first philosophy."

We can see, then, in the movement of the *Cartesian Meditations* up to this point, the expression of a certain hermeneutic principle. Husserl has projected a basic framework, in terms of the prebeginning, which will make possible and give determinate significance to the initial question of philosophy. This prebeginning, as a projection, is something which we have given to ourselves. It is not, however, the result of an arbitrary fiat of the will. The resolve to science, from Husserl's perspective, is nothing other than the recognition of one's own inherent rationality, and the willingness to come to terms with the absolute self-responsibility implied therein.

It is crucial to see the importance of the way in which the beginning question of philosophy is posed. The concern with the motives, or lack thereof, behind the transcendental turn in Husserl's phenomenology, is a theme which is often treated in phenomenological circles. But in the *Cartesian Meditations* we find the explicit posing of a question which will be the motivational force underlying the entire philosophical project. And it is the question of that which is first in itself, a question inherent in the very activity of science. In this question we find the germ of the whole of transcendental phenomenology.

That which makes the question possible, the prebeginning, is the idea of science concretely articulated in terms of evidence. The question sets us on the path to that evidence which is first in itself. At some point along this path, as we shall discover, the transcendental turn must be effected. There may indeed be no specific problem which could motivate such a radical break with the world. But what circumscribes all such particular problems is the problem of reason; its being true to itself and its own demands. Only an absolute commitment to rationality could lead to an absolute "denial" of the world. But this is something with which we shall have to deal later. For the present, it suffices to call attention to the crucial significance of a correct understanding of the beginning question. The answer to

"edifice of knowledge"

epistemic force = certainty

transcendental realm

the question leads to the transcendental realm, and our understanding of the very sense of the "transcendental" of phenomenology will be corrupt unless the question to which it is a response is worked out adequately.

There are three different forms in which the question of the beginning is formulated in the "First Meditation." The differences between the three can be comprehended as a movement from a less toward a more definite presentation of the question. First,

there emerges, as the question of the beginning, the inquiry for those cognitions that are first in themselves and can support the whole storied edifice of universal knowledge.[48]

The second way in which the question posed is in terms of the recognition that

we meditators, while completely destitute of all scientific knowledge, must have access to evidences that already bear the stamp of fitness for such a function, in that they are recognizable as preceding all other imaginable evidences.[49]

This is to say that the evidences which are to support the "edifice of knowledge" must have a precedence; that is, they must be first in themselves. In a marginal note to this passage, Husserl exclaims, "As founding evidences! And absolutely certain."[50]

The first formulation of the question has a strikingly Cartesian ring. There seems to be a definite epistemological tone, insofar as the notion of firstness is related to an edifice of knowledge. The way in which these evidences precede the derivative forms is with respect to certainty, to epistemic force. The second formulation can serve to reinforce this interpretation. However, Husserl's marginal note casts some light, or perhaps some shadows, upon the way in which "preceding" is to be interpreted. In this note, he draws a distinction between the *founding* character of evidence, and the *absolute certainty*. Can we collapse this distinction, or at least minimalize it, by seeing "founding" as epistemological in nature?

The relationship between our order of cognitions can be viewed as an epistemic relationship, strung out along the lines of degrees of certainty. Yet this is not the sense which "founding" has in Husserl's phenomenology. The concept of foundation is one which is first presented in the *Logical Investigations*, in particular, in regard to a formal theory of wholes and parts. In other words, the notion of founding belongs to a formal theory of objects, or formal ontology. The concept of foundation is one which arises in an a priori theory of objects, and not in the confines of an a priori or a posteriori theory of knowledge. However, the relationship between a theory of knowledge and a theory of objects remains questionable in Husserl, at least prior to the development of transcendental phenomenology; for up to that point, it is thought exclusively in naturalistic terms. This is a theme with which the next chapter will deal extensively. For now it should be noted, nonetheless, that there is reason for abstaining from any facile appropriation of the question of beginnings in terms of epistemic content alone.

These two tentative ways of presenting the question of the beginning finally give way to

> an initial *definite* question of beginning philosophy, the question whether it is possible for us to bring out evidences that, on the one hand, carry with them—as we now must say: apodictically— the insight that, as "first in themselves," they precede all other imaginable evidences, and, on the other hand, can be seen to be themselves apodictic.[51]

This formulation gives us a much clearer view of the notion of the evidences that are to serve as true beginnings. They must be "first in themselves" (a "foundational" precedence), and their "firstness" must be seen apodictically. Certain evidences may claim to provide absolute foundations. All such claims must be critically examined in light of the standard of apodicticity. Finally, the evidences themselves must be apodictic, that is, with regard not to their foundational capacities, but with respect to their intrinsic content as cognitions.

The question of the beginning, therefore, is a question bearing on evidence. We are searching for evidences that are both founding, and absolutely certain in a dual sense. The content of the evidential experiences must be absolutely certain, as must also be their priority or founding character. Evidence, as a universal characteristic of human experiencing, belongs to both scientific and prescientific life. Philosophy, as scientific striving, cannot rest content with relative evidences which suffice for everyday conduct. A certain perfection of evidence is requisite, and in this regard, Husserl claims that "at this decisive point in the process of beginning, we must penetrate deeper with our meditations."[52]

The perfection of evidence demanded by science differentiates itself into two related, yet distinguishable forms: apodictic evidence and adequate evidence. Husserl says that imperfection in evidence usually signifies incompleteness. Our experiences (evidences) are permeated with expectant components. We always mean something more than we "bodily" see. This is the tension between presence and absence which generates the movement of consciousness in the form of syntheses of identity. One form of perfection, therefore, would be a complete fulfillment of all anticipations. It would involve the conquering of all horizons, and more radically, the transcendence of the horizonal character of consciousness and world, analogous to the Kantian *archetypus intellectus*.

This idea, "that we shall become like gods," continually motivates the activity of inquiry. Yet another form of perfection, apodicticity, has an even higher dignity. Apodictic evidence

discloses itself, to a critical reflection, as having the signal peculiarity of being at the same time the absolute unimaginableness of their nonbeing, and thus excluding in advance every doubt as "objectless," empty.[53]

To secure apodictic evidence, in other words, requires both a straightforward attention to the givenness of an object or state of affairs, as well as a critical reflection which reveals (apodictically) that the given, in principle, could not be otherwise. Experience stands in need of criticism, as does the criticism itself. This dual criticism generates the twofold task of a complete phenomenology presented in Paragraph 13.

THE BEGINNING OF PHILOSOPHY

We have now traversed two dimensions of the task of beginning philosophy, as an introduction to phenomenology. The prebeginning phase led to a will to live truthfully under the idea of rationality understood in terms of intuition. This resolve produced the formulation of a question related to beginning evidences, evidences that are first in themselves *and* apodictic. How is it, then, that Husserl begins his search for such evidences? That is, how does phenomenology begin in the *Cartesian Meditations*?

Husserl initiates his phenomenological reflection with the response to the question which seems self-evident, namely, that evidence which is genuinely first in itself is supplied by the existence of the world. This is to say that the pregiven existence of the world is the foundation for all human enterprises, including philosophy. Each human activity is circumscribed by its worldly character. Both the scientific and prescientific life-function within the horizon of the already existing world, and can be comprehended as responses to the pregiven world. Strive as it might to transcend infinitely the limited convictions and relative evidences of ordinary life, science always returns to that life, both as the source of its primordial verifications, and as the subject matter which its constructions are intended to explain. "More than anything else, the being of the world is obvious."[54]

The tendency towards grounds in the philosophy of Husserl, as expressed in the beginning question of philosophy, seems to find its termination in the world. To say that the world is the "primary evidence" is to say nothing about its epistemological status, understood in terms of degrees of certainty. It is to affirm the world as the whole to which all other contents relate, either mediately or immediately. It is to say that all experiences (evidences), both sensuous and categorial, are worldly insofar as they select out some part as focus of an attentive gaze, which, when subject to a greater, critical attentiveness, is seen as part of that whole, that is, is seen within the limits of its givenness.

This answer to the question of philosophy, however, is unacceptable. It initially presents itself under the guise of its primacy or "firstness." Husserl's immediate criticism of this evidence, however, is with regard to its character as apodictic.

> But however much this evidence is *prior* in itself to all the other evidences of life (as turned toward the world) and to all the evidences of all the world sciences (since it is the basis that continually supports them), we soon become doubtful about the extent to which, in this capacity, it can lay claim to being *apodictic*.[55]

This "doubt" constitutes the second moment of the Cartesian way to the reduction.[56] For many interpreters of Husserl, it is *the* animating idea underlying the thrust of his phenomenology. Its importance cannot indeed be underestimated, for the radical denial of the world really provides the basis, for example, for the split between realism and idealism in phenomenology. And it also seems, at this juncture, that the departure from realism is necessitated solely by an episte-mological demand.[57]

Even if it were possible to surrender our belief in the existence of the world, why should we sacrifice it in the name of apodicticity? Why should we renounce the distinctively human character of experience at all levels, as that which furnishes it with its richness of content and even with its meaning, for some small, discernible core of truth, which might be as lacking in richenss and "life" as it is full in epistemic content? Why should epistemology, rather than ontology, assume the status of first philosophy?[58]

These objections, however, are groundless if we pay careful attention to the distinctions which Husserl himself draws in the text. For he goes on to say,

> if we follow up this *doubt* (i.e., with regard to the apodictic character of the world), it becomes *manifest* that our experiential evidence of the world lacks also the superiority of being the absolutely primary evidence.[59] (Italics mine.)

Here "absolute" refers to the characteristic of "firstness" rather than certainty. The initial claim put forward is that the pregiven existence of the world is the original and primordially founding basis for all human experiencing. Both its certainty and founding character are naively self-evident, even to the extent that "no one would think of asserting it expressly in a proposition."[60] Husserl now suggests, however, that it is *doubtful* whether or not this evidence satisfies the demand of perfection in apodicticity, while it becomes *manifest* that this evidence fails in terms of "firstness." At no point in the "First Meditation" does Husserl carry out a systematic denial of the apodictic character of world experience. He notes both particular instances of sensuous experience, as well as networks of sensuous experience which suffer devaluation. His conclusion from these examples, however, is very limimted.

> We need not take the indicating of these possible and sometimes actual reversals of evidence as a sufficient criticism of the evidence in question and see in it a full proof that, in spite of the continual experiencedness of the world, a non-being of the world is conceivable. We shall retain only this much: that the evidence of the world-experience would, at all events, need to be criticized with regard to its validity and range, before it could be used

for the purpose of a radical grounding of science, and that therefore we must not take that evidence to be, without question, immediately apodictic.[61]

The apodictic character of evidence, as we have noted above, demands a critical reflection for its recognition; one which exludes *in advance* the conceivability of doubt. What Husserl puts forward in the *Cartesian Meditations* is the claim that, prior to such a critical reflection, any insight into apodicticity is impossible. What is needed, therefore, is criticism of world-experience, and moreover, of the essence of world-experience. What belongs to the essence of any particular world-experience is its worldly character: that it selects out a part of the world. Prior to such a criticism, the world and all which it founds can have only the status of an "acceptance-phenomenon."

There are a variety of ways in which Husserl might proceed from this point. Surely the most obvious is to carry out such a criticism. But the hypothetical (imaginative-eidetic) annihilation of the world, such as was attempted in *Ideas I*, does not occur. Husserl, it is true, anticipates the result, but only in a hypothetical fashion, in order to pose a problem. And that problem has to do with the *intrinsic priority* of the world. What Husserl asks, as remarkable as it may sound, is for a way of avoiding the criticism of world-experience as the first task of philosophy.

Is not "the world" the name for the universe of whatever exists? If so, how can we avoid starting *in extenso*, and as our first task, that criticism of world-experience which, a moment ago, we merely indicated?[62]

If we could not avoid the task of criticism of world-experience, as the first task of philosophy, and *if* it resulted in the denial of the apodictic certainty of the world, and *if* the world is that which is intrinsically prior, does this not undermine the possibility of philosophy as rigorous science?

It seems as if the approach here should be the Cartesian one: that is, a demonstration of the lack of apodicticity of world experience accompanied by the insight that the *ego cogito* is in principle indubitable. Husserl explicitly says at this point, "following Descartes we make the great reversal."[63] This reversal, "if made in the right manner, leads to transcendental subjectivity."[64] The first glimpse of transcendental subjectivity in the *Cartesian Meditations* appears here, and Husserl's characterization of it is easily misinterpreted. Transcendental subjectivity is referred to as the *ego cogito*, as "the ultimate and apodictically certain basis for judgments, the basis on which any radical philosophy must be grounded."[65] Is this not precisely the establishment of the primacy of the ego on the ground of its perfection of evidence (apodicticity)? Is this not to say that the subject is *first* because it is more certain than the object; because it is given with apodicticity while the object and the world are merely assertoric?

To refute this tempting interpretation, we need only look to the author's marginal note, clarifying the sense in which apodicticity can be predicated of the transcendental subject at this level.

> It is necessary to say that the reduction has apodictic significance, since it shows apodictically that the being of the transcendental ego is antecedant to the being of the world.[66]

In other words, the apodictic insight has to do neither with the Being of the ego nor the Being of the world, but with the relationship between the two! That relationship is one of "antecedance." It is one of "firstness" or priority. The transcendental turn is not ushered in via the apodictic insight into the apodictic character of the "I am." To claim that the Being of the ego is antecedant to the Being of the world amounts to undermining the priority of the world as the whole. That to which all else relates (the relative), while it itself relates to nothing (the absolute), is not the world, but subjectivity seen transcendentally.[67] What this exhibits is that the transcendental character of Husserl's philosophy is not dependent upon the apodictic character of the ego, although its claim to be science may well be.

Two points should now be made with regard to the component of apodicticity in the ideal of science. These bear on the dual sense of apodicticity which was mentioned above.[68] The first has to do with the extent to which the priority of subjectivity over the world naively understood has been established. In Paragraph 8, Husserl attempts to give us a glimpse of transcendental subjectivity, not with respect to its concrete content, nor regarding its eidetic structures, but simply into its nature as transcendental.[69] This is to say nothing other than that the ego, when seen in its purity, is that which is "first in itself" as ground of the world. We shall quote the entire concluding paragraph of the section in which transcendental subjectivity is introduced in order to reinforce this point.

Thus the being of the pure ego and his *cogitationes*, as a being
that is prior in itself, is antecedant to the natural being of the
world—the world of which I always speak, the one of which I
can speak. Natural being is a realm whose existential status
(*Seinsgeltung*) is secondary; it continually presupposes the realm
of transcendental being. The fundamental phenomenological
method of transcendental *epoche*, because it leads back to this
realm, is called transcendental-phenomenological reduction.[70]

We can see, then, that the sense of the transcendental in Husserl
has simply to do with the way in which we think the relationship
between ego and world. Here Husserl expresses the transcendental
insight in claiming that the ego is "prior in itself," "antecedant,"
and "continually presupposed." What these terms mean more concretely will be the subject matter of the following chapter.

It ought to be remembered that the insight into this relationship
should be an apodictic one, for it is in that sense alone that the
reduction has apodictic significance. Husserl qualifies the entire presentation of the reduction in Paragraph 8 with the following marginal
note: "There seems to be lacking the apodicticity of the precedence
belonging to transcendental subjectivity."[71] Apodicticity involves the
a priori recognition of absolute necessity; that a given state of affairs
could not be otherwise, in principle. In questioning the apodicticity
of the precedence belonging to transcendental subjectivity, Husserl
is actually calling into question the *necessity* of the transcendental
turn itself.

It was suggested in the opening pages of this chapter, as a possible
interpretation, that the only motive which can be uncovered for
transcendental phenomenology lies in the initial, absolute commitment to the rational absolute. An apodictic insight into the "firstness"
of the ego would disclose that necessity of thinking the self transcendentally. Insights into necessity, however, are eidetic insights,
attained via the process of imaginative variation. What would be
required, therefore, for apodicticity vis-a-vis this relation would be
the recognition that all other attempts at being reasonable lead, in
principle, to *aporiai.*

This would be one way of understanding the importance of the
Crisis. There Husserl tries to interpret transcendental phenomenology
as the final realization of the sense of modern philosophy. By running
through various historical forms of reason, and showing that they
must fail in that they share the common prejudice of the precedence

of the world as the ultimate horizon of meaning, Husserl hopes to establish the necessity of the transcendental turn, just insofar as one retains a commitment to reason. The history of philosophy appears as its own slaughterbench, in that it necessarily terminates in the "paradox of human subjectivity."[72] In other words, there may be an inherent shortcoming in the Cartesian way to transcendental phenomenology, as Husserl explicitly notes in the *Crisis*. But the rejection of this way is not based upon its overly epistemological character, for such a character was never present. Rather, it breaks down in its failure to disclose the apodictic precedence of the ego over the world, and hence the inherent necessity of the transcendental turn.

The second remark on apodicticity involves the recognition of the apodictic character of the Being of the "I am." This is the third and final component of the question of true beginnings, and it is introduced as the "next question,"[73] consequent to the establishment of the primacy of the ego. It is with regard to this aspect of phenomenology that Husserl follows Cartesian thought most closely. For Descartes also grasped the Being of the ego as apodictic. But *what* this ego is, and in *what sense it is*, still remained problematic.

Husserl recognizes manifold difficulties with regard to the apodictic givenness of the ego to itself. The lived experiences of the ego, like the objects in the world given through experience, have a horizonal character. The structures of presence and absence permeate the "I" as well as the "non-I"; and these structures provide the background for the dynamic of fulfillment and cancellation, which is the movement or achieving activity of evidence itself. The way in which the past belongs to the ego, as well as its habitualities, discloses that "yet to be fulfilled" components are involved in transcendental self-consciousness as well. Husserl says that the apodicticity of the "I am" is still secure, "though not as yet what determines its being more particularly and is still not itself given, but only presumed during the living evidence of the I-am."[74] The experience of negative evidence with regard to the Being of transcendent objects can always negate that Being, cancelling it into mere illusion. The horizonal character of self-experience also necessarily contains the possibility of negative evidence, yet any such occurrence is incapable of cancelling the Being of the experiencing ego itself, in its living presence.

In the "Second Meditation," Husserl claims that phenomenology must indeed proceed in two stages; first, the exploration of the transcendental ego, and second, criticism of transcendental experience itself, through which the ego is given. The science of phenomenology elicits the universal structures of transcendental life. Husserl claims that these, along with the bare "I am" are apodictically given. This, however, points to the task of criticism just insofar as we move beyond the living present. Such criticism, however, belongs to a higher stage, presupposing an initial naivete in which we live straightforwardly in the expeiences. But this higher stage is not to be found in the *Cartesian Meditations*.

What conclusions can we now draw with regard to the beginning of phenomenology in the *Cartesian Meditations*? The life of reason, whose highest value lies in the radical self-autonomy of the individual, seeks, according to Husserl, absolute rational grounds. This ideal was articulated in terms of beginning evidences, which had three different characteristics:

1. That they be "first in themselves"
2. That their "firstness" be apodictically certain
3. That their content as well be apodictic

All three of these are inseparable moments of the ideal of science, and from Husserl's perspective, the surrender of any one of them leads to the annihilation of science, of reason, and ultimately of spirit itself. These constitute the essence of science.

But the way in which these elements constitute the essence of science is as an ideal toward which we live. Science as a cultural fact and scientific activity within a culture exist. Yet science has not realized itself in its scientific character in a constitutive manner. Nowhere is there Science, but only the will to science, and the products of this will (sciences). The same is true of transcendental phenomenology as we find it introduced in the *Cartesian Meditations*. Only one of the components of the essence of science has been realized; namely, the discovery of the intrinsic priority of the self. This has not, however, been established apodictically, nor has the range of apodictic evidence of the ego been established. Yet nonetheless we have a transcendental phenomenology.

In other words, if the transcendental turn has been carried out; and if we really do have the transcendental ego by the end of the "First Meditation," so that we can go on to "lay out the field of transcendental experience";[75] and if, at the same time, the apodictic components of the ideal of science have yet to be realized; then we must conclude that the essence of transcendental phenomenology, insofar as this essence is constitutive, cannot include apodicticity as one of its moments.

Let us try to clarify this further. A distinction must be drawn between essences which are constitutive, and essences which are regulative. This need not be taken as a distinction between two discrete entities, but more in their function with respect to human activity. All science embodies the essence of science as a claim. Otherwise, it would have been impossible to uncover this essence via an immersion in scientific striving. In fact, however, no science embodies any of the components of science in a constitutive fashion. With Husserl, the science of transcendental phenomenology makes its appearance de facto. As a science, it strives toward this ideal, and perhaps in the most radical fashion possible. Constitutive for the existence of transcendental phenomenology, however, is the attainment of that which is first in itself, the fulfillment of the initial component of the essence of science. The specifically transcendental character of Husserl's phenomenology, therefore, lies not in its securing of apodicticity, for this remains a task for a higher stage of transcendental phenomenology.

Husserl's turn to the subject, therefore, must be concretely differentiated from that of his predecessors in modern philosophy. Descartes turns to the self because he recognizes the indubitability of the *cogito*. An instance of genuine knowledge will allow us to extract the criteria for knowledge, namely clarity and distinctness, and apply these to the problem of knowing the world. Thus the first task for Descartes is the reintroduction of the world, now in mathematical terms, based upon the criteria of clarity and distinctness. Kant situates the a priori on the side of the subject, for only in that way will the universality and necessity of knowledge be preserved against the onslaught of a strict empiricism.[76] We can move from unrestricted generality to the consciousness of eidetic necessity (apodicticity) only if the a priori is "subjective."[77]

Husserl's philosophy, however, subordinates the apodictic quest to that of firstness." The ideal of apodicticity is nowhere denied, yet the transcendental turn is not undertaken in its name alone. If it were, it would have to be evaluated as a complete failure.[78] And this interpretation is not uncommon. What is suggested here, however, is that the transcendental dimension be comprehended in its own specific nature prior to such cirticism. In the next chapter, we shall turn to a more comprehensive interpretation of the transcendental nature of Husserl's thought, in terms of a kind of "logic of the phenomenological reduction." Then, and only then, can we begin an evaluation of phenomenology as transcendental idealism.

3
Toward a Logic of the Transcendental Reduction

hierarchy of evidences

I N THE PRECEDING PAGES, we have come to see that for Husserl, the task of science and the task of philosophy, the most radical science, is to return to "the things themselves." At the very core of science is the concept of evidence, or more precisely, of a hierarchy of evidences. Gadamer is correct, for example, in claiming that Husserl views the task of phenomenology as residing precisely in the exposition of this hierarchy.[1] The way in which evidences relate to each other, as determinative for their hierarchical character, is crucial in the articulation of the things themselves. It was the mistake, for example, of Cartesian rationalism to view this relationship as geometric or deductive. Such a procedure illegitimately imposes upon the totality of beings a methodological ideal derived from a certain region, without a preparatory consideration of whether the objects of other regions give themselves in a fashion which admits of, and demands, such a methodology. Husserl's phenomenology hopes to avoid this kind of prejudice by a strict allegiance to the principle of givenness and the limitations contained therein.

One of the primary results of our analyses of the movement into the transcendental sphere has been that the notion of hierarchy belonging to evidences is not simply that of degrees of epistemic force. The way in which evidences relate, the order which they intrinsically possess as evidences, bifurcates into that tending toward apodicticity on the one hand, and toward "firstness" or founding on the other. The ideal of science involves the apodictic insight into the apodictic nature of the founding evidences, as well as into their foundational character.

From the phenomenological point of view, the quest for apodicticity takes place at a higher level: a metaphenomenology which furnishes a critique of phenomenological experience itself. The transcendental nature of phenomenology, however, is secured with the insight into the founding character of the evidences given in transcendental experience. Whether transcendental phenomenology can realize the full ideal of science remains problematic at this stage.

It thus seems impossible to situate the transcendental motif exclusively, or even primarily, in the quest for an apodictic evidence. The apodictic and the founding cannot simply be identified. Even if we ascribe such an identification to Descartes, this is possible only to the extent that the apodictic would function as an axiom for deductions. The founding character of the apodictic in Cartesianism lies in its axiomtic nature, apodicticity being external to its foundational capacity per se. Ideally, all axioms would be apodictic. But not all apodictic evidences need be axioms.

There has been considerable talk in the preceding pages about that which is first in itself, that which is a ground, or which functions as the primordial foundation. This has been undertaken in the name of clarifying the sense of the transcendental in phenomenology. Husserl himself says:

All justifications have their final source and their unity in the unity of the knowing and transcendentally pure subjectivity. Thus, a science of origins, a first philosophy, a science of transcendental subjectivity is required.[2]

Most of what we have said regarding these foundations or grounds has been negative. Much labor was expended on differentiating the notion of "firstness" characteristic of transcendental phenomenology from that of the primordiality of an evidence which is in itself apodictic. What is now required is a clarification of the sense in which Husserl can legitimately claim that subjectivity is antecedent to all objective reality. It is, at least in part, in the nature of this antecedance that subjectivity wins the status of absolute Being.

The sense of the transcendental is a relational one, in that its meaning can be comprehended only as a term standing in relationship to the transcendent. This is clear in both *Idea I* and the *Cartesian Meditations*. The inversion of the meaning of Being which results from the eidetic analysis of consciousness undertaken in *Ideas I*, testifies to an essential relationship between the transcendent and the transcendental.[3] In the *Cartesian Meditations*, Husserl legitimates the use of the term "transcendental" precisely by claiming that the domain of subjectivity is "presupposed" by the transcendent.[4] The task that we set ourselves in this chapter is the uncovering of the precise nature of this relationship through a careful study of the sense in which precedence or "firstness" can be attributed to subjectivity. This, in turn, will be brought about in such a fashion that the unity of the presentations of the transcendental reduction undertaken in the two previous chapters will be firmly established.

Moreover, the fundamental unity of the entire Husserlian project, the continuity of the pretranscendental with the transcendental period, will be thrown into clearer relief. The establishment of such an inner unity discloses the transcendental reduction, not as a betrayal of the original impetus of Husserl's phenomenology, but rather as merely a variation and logical extension of the eidetic reduction. It is a special kind of eidetic reduction, one in which what I shall later term "eidetic rationality" completes itself.

THE CONCEPT OF FOUNDATION

The most general term that might be applied to the relationship between subjectivity and objectivity from Husserl's transcendental perspective is that of ground or foundation. Up to this point, this relationship has been characterized in a privative manner only; namely, that it is not primordially a question of the apodictic versus the nonapodictic. Can we say anything positive about this new and unique idea of ground or foundation? In order to do this, we shall have to return to a much earlier work of Husserl's in which he introduced the notion of foundation, the *Logical Investigations*. It is in the third of these Investigations, in the "theory of wholes and parts," that Husserl first presents the idea of foundation, giving it a precise definition, and using it to explicate the variety of relations functioning between parts and wholes. We know that Husserl himself placed great emphasis on this Investigation, claiming it to be both "too little read [and] an essential presupposition for the full understanding of the Investigations which follow."[5] I would suggest that it is not only essential for the remaining sections of the *Logical Investigations*, but for all phenomenological studies, including those of transcendental phenomenology itself.[6]

The context within which the notion of foundation is introduced is that of "the pure (a priori) theory of objects as such."[7] It begins with the consideration of Stumpf's distinction between independent and dependent contents and attempts to move beyond the framework of a psychological analysis of the contents of consciousness to objective truths about an object as such, a "something in general."[8] Husserl insists that the sorts of relationships which will be investigated here "have an a priori foundation in the idea of an object."[9] In other words, the way in which we think these relations is not the product of an empirical or factual necessity (in the limited sense of generality) grounded in the psychological structure of human thinking, but rather is dictated by the objects themselves. The study of logic must be independent of all branches of anthropology, including psychology.

The entire investigation of wholes and parts is directed toward the *relations* which can exist among parts, as well as between parts and wholes. It is in terms of relation that the distinction is drawn between independent (*selbstandigen*) and nonindependent or dependent (*unselbstandigen*) objects. This difference corresponds to that between pieces and moments. The distinction is only terminological.

In the second chapter of the third Investigation, Husserl begins with a definition of foundation and in light of that offers "exact determinations of the concepts of Piece, Moment, Physical Part, Abstractum, Concretum."[10] The most primordial relationship that can hold among parts, or objects in general, is that of foundation, and it is in terms of its presence or absence that the distinction is drawn between different kinds of parts. In Paragraph 14 of Investigation III, Husserl gives the following definition of foundation:

> If a law of essence means that an *A* cannot as such exist except in a more comprehensive unity which associates it with an *M*, we say that an *A* as such requires foundation by an *M*, or also that an *A* as such needs to be supplemented by an *M*.[11]

The relationship of foundation can assume a variety of forms: for example, reciprocal or one-sided, mediate or immediate. Thus, Husserl gives the examples of color and visual extension as reciprocally or mutually founding, while a judgment is one-sidedly founded on its presentations. Presentations are possible without judgments, but judgments without presentations are impossible. Color is immediately founded on visual extension, while brightness is mediately founded, via color, on extension.

However, what is significant here is not the mere enumeration of these differences between foundational relations per se. Instead, we wish to look to "the most remarkable differences among the *a priori* relationships holding between whole and part, and among the parts of one and the same whole."[12] Husserl goes on to say:

> Not every part is included in its whole in the same fashion, and not every part is woven together with every other, in the unity of a whole, in the same way . . . . A hand, for example, forms part of a person in quite a different way from the color of his hand, from his body's total extent, from his mental acts, and from the internal "moments" of such phenomena.[13]

These differences are derivative from the concept of foundation, and give rise to the general distinction between pieces and moments.

> We first perform a fundamental division of the concept part into *pieces*, or parts in the narrowest sense, and into *moments* or *abstract parts* of the whole. Each part that is independent relatively to a whole W we call a piece (portion), and each part that is non-independent relatively to W we call a moment (an abstract part) of this same whole.[14]

We can see, therefore, that in a certain sense, the relationship of foundation is one that functions only within the domain of moments or abstract parts (*abstracta*). For the definition of foundation points to the presence of an essential relationship between elements or objects such that the condition for the possibility of the objects' existence lies in their necessary correlation with other objects.

The relationship between whole and part on the side of formal ontology corresponds with that between substrate and determination in the realm of formal apophantics. The exact parallel between the two disciplines, for Husserl, makes is possible for us to move back and forth between the two in the following pages.[15] On the side of the object, all parts necessarily refer back to the wholes of which they are parts; while with respect to apophantics, as a theory of judgments, all determinations refer back to substrates. The essential divisions on both sides between kinds of parts, independent and nonindependent, therefore, testify to a correlative differentiation between types of wholes.

This is to say that certain wholes require a distinct moment of unity, insofar as the parts that compose those wholes are independent, lacking any essential relation to one another. With respect to wholes that can be broken down into pieces, the need for moments of unity is "obvious and indispensable a priori."[16] If we think, for example, of a line of people, then insofar as that object is to be grasped as such, and not as a simple aggregate or set, a distinctive form of unity is required. But this is not the case with all objects or wholes; "there need not be a specific 'moment' of unity which binds all the parts."[17] Those wholes whose parts are moments, essentially dependent, require no external bond.

All talk of unifying presupposes antecedent separation. But with regard to moments, such prior separation is a priori impossible. It could only be the result of fundamentally confused and abstract thinking, in isolation from all contact with intuitive giveness, that could produce the demands, and consequently undertake the task, of bringing together that which is *essentially* one. For in this case, the objects

> are in fact "founded" on one another, and for this reason they require no chains or bonds to chain or knit them together, or to bring them to one another. In their case all these expressions have in fact no sense at all. Where it makes nonsense to speak of isolation, the problem of overcoming such isolation is likewise nonsensical.[18]

From Husserl's position, some of the most significant and vexing philosophical dilemmas have arisen from just such a nonsensical demand. Perhaps the most damaging of these has been the separation of subject and object, consciousness and world, and the epistemological task of reuniting them. Husserl wants to claim that such a problematic could have arisen only insofar as the point of departure for philosophical activity was infected with prejudices, insofar as one began with language and thought, rather than with an attentive intuitional regard for that which is given within the limits of its givenness.

A descriptive method, rooted in intuition, need not surrender to any explanatory onsets insofar as it has for its objects moments standing in a priori interconnectedness, and not pieces in need of synthesis via the introduction of third terms. From the perspective of Husserl's phenomenology, what is involved here is not a facile dismissal of any legitimate problematics, but the recognition of the fundamentally illegitimate and misdirected nature of all attempts to synthesize that which is one in essence. Such original unity is not posited after the fact, so as to make solutions possible, but is given with the objectivity of the object itself. Being truthful demands submission in light of such givenness.

Phenomenology, therefore, whether transcendental or not, as an eidetic science, will limit itself to the description and explication of wholes vis-a-vis their dependent parts. These parts, of course, always lead us back to the wholes of which they are the parts. Such wholes, in turn, (or on the side of apophantics, substrates) can themselves be parts and correlatively can bifurcate into pieces (*concreta*) and moments (*abstracta*). A moment of piece would be the color belonging to a man's hand, while a moment of a moment might be the brightness of the color, or the smoothness of the surface.

What Husserl claims is that our analyses cannot remain within the domain of the dependent ad infinitum. At some point the relationship between moment and that of which it is a moment (a relative whole, or *concretum*) must terminate in an independent object. This might be a piece of some other object, but it must, in principle, be capable of independent existence and presentation to consciousness. We we reach this level we have discovered an absolute *concretum*. Husserl explains this notion by stating: "A concretum that itself is abstract in no direction can be called an 'absolute concretum'."[19]

In *Experience and Judgment*, Husserl attempts to establish the same claims, only proceeding from the side of apophantics rather than formal ontology.

> The continuing relativization *in infinitum* of the distinction between substrate and determination in the course of experience has its limits, and we must come to distinguish between substrates and determinations in an absolute sense.[20]

Basically, Husserl here argues that while determinations can indeed become substrates and function as such, via "substratification," not all substrates can arise in such a fashion. For the movement from determination to substrate presupposes an original substrate for which the determination was a determination. These substrates which are not the result of any substratification, but are given prior to such activity, and supply the basis for all such predicative acts, are called absolute substrates.

An absolute substrate, therefore, is distinguished in this way, that it is simply and directly experienceable, that it is immediately apprehensible, and that its explication can immediately be brought into play.[21]

We can see, therefore, that the idea of foundation applies not only to moments considered as parts, and hence in terms of the relation of part to part, but also to the structure of whole and part. That which is necessarily nonindependent is a moment of that which is independent, either mediately or immediately. Thus the relation between a whole and its parts, when the latter are moments, is a foundational relationship, in that insofar as a moment "is" at all, it is as a nonindependent part of some whole. If we think of visual extension, for example, we must also think of some color, and hence a relationship of foundation exists. But furthermore, we can only think the extension as that of some thinglike object which is extended, and which has extension as an essential part, that is, as a moment.[22]

 What is being pointed to here is confirmed, for example, in the idea that all essential intuition begins with an individual, and via a process of imaginative variation, can arrive at that which characterized the individual essentially, its pure *eidos*. Beginning with an individual, however, does not presuppose its existential status as a being in the world, and existing as such, as a spatio-temporally individuated object of possible sensous experience. Essences are essentially "essences of", as individual objects, qua objects, are essentially "instances of."[23]

TRANSCENDENTAL SUBJECTIVITY AS ABSOLUTE *Concretum*

But even if we draw such a variety of distinctions between different types of parts and wholes, along with the levels of mediacy and immediacy, it is still difficult to see how such concepts have an applicability beyond the spheres of formal ontology in general, and the various material, regional eidetics. Such ideas may indeed be useful and even necessary as a logic for the working out of material ontologies. They might very well stand at the core of the programs executing the work of phenomenology conceived in terms of a realist orientation toward essential Being. But how can we claim that such concepts illuminate the most fundamental significance of the transcendental reduction? How can they supply a guiding clue for comprehending the sense of "firstness" attributed to transcendental subjectivity?

One of the consequences of Husserl's analysis of wholes and parts in the third Investigation is that an essential distinction is drawn between types of parts, such that we recognize an eidetic necessity inherent in certain objects and species of objects which compels them to be parts. The distinction between independent and dependent objects illuminates the essentially fragmentary nature of the Being of certain objects. All dependent objects can *exist* only in a more comprehensive unity, that is, only as parts of some whole. Pieces, on the other hand, are merely contingently parts. As independent objects, they may *in fact* only exist in more comprehensive unities. But such a mode of Being is a factual state of affairs, whose truth or falsity always stands in need of further verification through experience. There is no essential relationship between pieces, and consequently the task of the discovery of the regular ordering and coherence of independent objects is reserved for the sciences of experience.

But the concept of foundation is precisely that which supplies the noematic basis of the method of eidetic intuition for all essential sciences. Imaginative variation is the vehicle through which we discover that certain objects can only be insofar as they are interconnected with others. Hence, it is this "interweaving of the Essences" which supplies limits to the imaginative process, limits which make possible rational, philosophical science. The foundational relation allows for "variation that is free, though not excluded by a law rooted in the content's essence."[24] Eidetic insight is possible solely on the basis of foundational relations existing among "objects in general."

The commitment to rationality, which was articulated in both *Ideas I* and the *Cartesian Meditations* (and is implicit in all of Husserl's works), entails a recognition that intuition, and that which is given "bodily" in intuition, must be accepted as it gives itself.[25] All claims against intuition would proceed in light of intuition, and consequently be contradictory in nature.[26] The recognition of the essentially partial or fragmentary nature of dependent objects points the intuitive (scientific-philosophical) consciousness to those more comprehensive unities to which the moments belong. Abstract thought can linger on the moments without noticing their essentially partial Being, as can, for example, all "abstractive" sciences of nature and spirit. But only if we return to that which gives itself within the limits of its givenness is it possible to avoid mistaking an *abstractum* for a *concretum*, and correlatively, a constructivistic beginning point for inquiry.

At some point in the course of analysis, therefore, we will be led back to those entities which are independent, standing in no essential relationship to other objects in the sense that they need supplementation or foundation for possible existence. Such objects, it would seem, could never be moments; they could not, in principle, be *founded* on anything else. Their relation to that which is other is only factual, standing beyond the sphere of any eidetic science, including phenomenology.

It is seemingly in this domain that we encounter those foundational relationships which are one-sided, rather than mutual. In such cases, the foundational content or object can be independent. In other words, with the discovery of independent objects, those wholes of which the moments are essentially parts, we find that which is founding but not founded. In the *Logical Investigations*, Husserl refers to these as the absolute *concreta*. In *Experience and Judgment*, these are the absolute substrates, or original object substrates. The latter are contrasted to the absolute determinations,

> to which the form of determination is essential, whose being must be characterized originally and on principle only as the being-such of another being. . . . A priori, they acquire the substrate form only by a specific activity making them independent. In this sense, absolute substrates are independent; absolute determinations are dependent.[27]

With the discovery of that which is founding, and not in turn founded, we seem to have come to the boundaries of eidetic investigations, to that which is indeed "first in itself." Is this not that which, "in principle *nulla 're' indiget ad existendum* (needs no other thing to exist)"?[28] Several questions need to be posed here. What are these absolute *concreta*? Are they one or many? How can we explicate the notion of genuine "firstness" via the insight into that which is founding but not founded? And what bearing, if any, does this have on the development of Husserl's transcendental philosophy?

In the *Logical Investigations*, Husserl does not specifically enumerate those objects which satisfy the criteria for being absolute *concreta*. He does assert that "a thing or piece of a thing"[29] fulfills such stipulations. Furthermore, the notion of independence characterizes

> phenomenal objects as such, as well as the appearances in the sense of the experiences, in which these things appear, as also in respect of the sensational complexes which are given an objective interpretation in such experiences.[30]

The specific example which Husserl utilizes to bring out the distinction between dependent and independent objects is that of a *the* · head of a horse as a piece of a thing which is a piece only de facto, and not essentially. Husserl claims that such objects "appear possible even if nothing whatever exist beside them, nothing therefore bound up with them to form a whole."[31]

"horizon"

The relationship between object and horizon, at the time of the *Logical Investigations*, is one which seems to fall outside the sphere of essential necessity. Husserl even suggests the logical possibility that our visual field could shrink down to some single content or independent object.[32] It is clear, then, that with respect to independent objects, Husserl minimizes the significance of the horizonal character, attributing it to a "subjective" or psychological necessity at best. Such a view is demanded by the nature of the relation functioning between part and whole in this context. This position, however, will alter radically with the onset of transcendental phenomenology, which responds to the world as the universal acceptance-horizon.

It is of considerable interest to note the language in which Husserl describes the independent character of the absolute *concreta* in the *Logical Investigations*, for it is a clear anticipation of the attributes accredited to pure consciousness, and to pure consciousness *alone*, once the transcendental turn is effected. For example, in Paragraphs 5 and 6 of Investigation III, Husserl says the following about the independent existence of absolute *concreta*:

In the "nature" of the content itself, in its ideal essence, no dependence on other contents is rooted; the essence that makes it what it is, also leaves it unconcerned with all other contents.[33]

In contrast to this, a dependent content (object), "is by its nature bound to other contents, it cannot be, if other contents are not there together with it."[34]

Furthermore, Husserl asserts:

A thing or piece of a thing can be presented by itself—this means it would be what it is even if everything outside it were annihiliated. If we form a presentation of it, we are not necessarily referred to something else, included in which, or attached to which, or associated with which, it has being, or on whose mercy it depends, as it were, for its existence.[35]

Again, thinglike contents (objects) can "be thought of as self-existent, as isolated from all else, as being all that exists. . . ."[36] And finally, in describing the difference between the independent and the dependent, Husserl says that the one "can be 'in and for itself,' while another can only have being in, or attached to, some other object."[37]

These passages should be compared, for example, with Section 49 of *Ideas I*, in which Husserl posits the absolute Being of consciousness precisely on the grounds of its *essential independence* from transcendent reality, while, "the world of the transcendent 'res' is related unreservedly to consciousness. . . ."[38] "Reality, that of the thing taken singly as also that of the whole world, essentially lacks independence."[39] With regard to the independence of consciousness, Husserl asserts:

> If conscious experiences were inconceivable apart from their interlacing with nature in the very way in which colors are inconceivable apart from extension, we could not look upon consciousness as an absolute region for itself alone in the sense in which we must actually do so. . . . It is essentially independent of all Being of the type of a world or Nature, and it has no need for these for its existence.[40]

What we find here is that the status of independent objects attributed to thinglike existents in the *Logical Investigations* is now attributed to consciousness, while transcendent entities, and the whole "real" world (the factworld), is essentially dependent, thinkable only as the correlate of such consciousness. Thus, in the *Cartesian Meditations*, Husserl, in reflecting on phenomenology as being necessarily transcendentally idealistic, claims:

> The attempt to conceive the universe of true being as lying somehow outside the universe of possible consciousness, possible knowledge, possible evidence, the two being related merely externally by a rigid law, is non-sensical. They belong together essentially, and, as belonging together essentially, they are also concretely one, one in *the only absolute concretion*: transcendental subjectivity.[41]

From these passages it is clear that the logic of wholes and parts is at work throughout Husserl's development and structures the very movement to transcendental phenomenology itself.

THING, WORLD, AND TRANSCENDENTAL SUBJECTIVITY

In order to make this "logic of the transcendental reduction" a little clearer, we shall work through a consideration of various possible absolute *concreta*, attempting to uncover the inner dynamic of the movement toward origins in the most radical sense in Husserl's thought. We shall progress through a consideration of the individual thing, the world, and finally transcendental subjectivity. The focal point shall be the movement from part to whole, in light of the demands of intuitive givenness, that is, the unfolding of eidetic rationality as it moves toward the transcendental turn.

It has often been noted that Husserl's thought, at the time of the *Logical Investigations*, is oriented fundamentally toward a phenomenological realism.[42] The majority of Husserl's earliest students refused to proceed to the level of transcendental idealism, a refusal which Husserl took to be rooted in a sort of dogmatic "ontologism" and realism.[43] It would seem that the passages which we cited from the *Logical Investigations* regarding the independent status of individual thinglike contents substantiates this realist thesis of the absolute existence of the transcendent thing. While general objects (essences) are essentially related to consciousness, individual objects can exist independently of any such relations. This simply gives expression to the fundamental thesis of the natural attitude. While this thesis is not articulated in the *Logical Investigations* as such, insofar as it is *natural*, it must be active.[44] At this stage, Husserl's concern is simply not aimed in this direction.

We can look, for example, to passages in *Formal and Transcendental Logic* in which Husserl describes the limited nature of the concerns of his phenomenology prior to the advent of the transcendental turn. The "Prolegomena to Pure Logic" in the *Logical Investigations* was a response to a limited epistemological problematic, rooted in the historical circumstances of the appearance of logical psychologism. The "irreal" formations of logic, its judgmental forms, inferences, arguments, proofs, categorial objects, and so forth, are recognized as correlates of specific kinds of conscious activities, and only as correlates of these conscious activities.

One does not come across a judgment in the world in the same way as one does a table, chair, or melody. Judgments refer back to judgings for their ontological status.

What accrues *originaliter* in the judicative doing as subjects and predicates, premise-propositions, conclusion-propositions, and so forth, does indeed make its appearance member by member, in the field of the judger's consciousness. It is nothing alien to the psychic, nothing like a physical process, a physical formation accruing in physical action.[45]

logical psychologism

Even when the distinction is made between the process or activity and the object which takes shape in it, that is, when the intentionality of consciousness is recognized, logical psychologism still results in the equating of the objectivity in question with that which appears in internal experience.

Such a position, however, is only a species of a "universal epistemological aberration, a universal epistemological psychologism,"[46] which is never brought into view in the *Logical Investigations*. Psychologistic temptations with regard to the real world of nature, of spatio-temporally individuated object, remain nonexistent. This holds, however, only due to a lack of serious reflection about the conditions for the possibility of knowledge of how "transcendence" is possible. More formally speaking, it persists only insofar as we abstract from the whole.

If we ask in what the independence of the absolute *concreta* consists, the answer is in their ability to maintain self-identity throughout the potentially infinite variation of the cogiven objects constituting the horizon. When this variation results in the destruction or annihilation of the self-sameness of the object, then the content or object which fostered this annihilation is seen as necessarily connected with the object in question, as *founding* it.

The conclusion that can be drawn from this is that only *momenta* are necessarily given with a horizon, the latter being the whole of which they are parts. When a moment is present, its whole is necessarily copresent, while when a piece or independent object is present, its whole is only contingently copresent.

The *Logical Investigations*, in attributing absolute existence to thing-like contents, by divorcing the horizon from the givenness of such objects, or relegating it to a conventional status, can be interpreted as a forgetting of the worldly character of individual entities.[47] From such a perspective the world is seen ony as a totality of beings, one-sidedly founded in the individual entities which populate it. The entities themselves can be thought, and can exist, independently of the world qua totality, in the same fashion that the individual presentations underlying a judgment can be independently of the judgment form. As Husserl later says, "the experience of the totality of nature is *founded* in the prior experiences of individual bodies."[48]

But this concept of the world, as totality, is not that which is presented as the correlate of the natural attitude. If the belief in the existence of the world were founded in the individual acts of world experience, then the suspension of that belief through the transcendental reduction could be effected only via an infinite "running through" which would neutralize each act. But this infinite task is not what the reduction calls for, since the latter is realized in "a single stroke."

The world as believed in cannot be the correlate of an ideal totality of acts; and the "worldly" character of individual objects cannot reside in their being pieces of such a totality. On the contrary, the belief in the existence of the world must found the belief in the existence of the individual objects, for a suspension of the former successfully suspends the latter. No second "parenthesizing" is necessary, in addition to the bracketing of the world, which would bracket the individual objects in the world. Objectively or noematiclly speaking, the world founds the objects in the world.[49]

To say this, however, is to say that individual objects in the world are *essentially parts of the world*, are *momenta* of the whole, world. This involves the denial of the status of absolute *concreta* attributed to the individual thing in the *Logical Investigations*. The self-identity of the absolute *concreta* must not be dependent upon any more comprehensive unity with which it is associated. With the introduction of the concept of the natural attitude, Husserl recognizes that the self-identity of the individual object is not simply pregiven in itself, but is dependent upon the belief in the existence of the world. Such a recognition leads to "a new understanding of the concept of absolute subtrate."[50] What is implied is

> that everything mundane, whether a real unity or a real plurality, is ultimately dependent; only the world is independent; only it is absolute substrate in the strict sense of absolute independence.[51]

The natural attitude claims that the foundation of beings, that which lets them be what they are, rests in the world as such.

The function of the world, therefore, in this context, is not merely that of a horizon of possible objects of further experience.[52] Such an image has its focal point or center of gravity in the particular determinate object grasped via an intentional act. This act and its object are saturated with actuality and possibility, as intuitively grasped and emptily intended. The "intuitive absence" of the emptily intended can constitute both internal and external horizons. But these horizons, the external one being the coapprehended whole, bear the significance of fields of possible research, activity, decision making, and so forth, which can be fulfilled in intentional acts executed along a motivational line from the present act and its objects to these fields. The world, then, would be the totality of beings or objects, in the broadest possible sense.

This image is incomplete, however, for it is only one-sided. The presence of the world as given and believed in by man living in the natural attitude is not only the presence of absent objects (i.e., possible objects), but is pregiven, and so infiltrates any individual experience that the very Being of the object of experience attains its ontological status from the world. The natural attitude implicitly contains an ontological thesis which ascribes objectivity to that which is given in experience precisely on the basis of its "being in the world." The world supplies the ground for the distinction between the "for us" and the "in itself." That which is "in itself" is the self-identical object to which we can return again and again in repeated acts. It is because of this self-identity that we ascribe objectivity and hence transcendence to such givens. Objects can be objects in themselves, and not only for us, precisely because they always belong to a world which is pregiven as present, "out there."

From the standpoint of the natural attitude, it is the world in its bestowing of worldliness upon entities which prevents the collapse of the "in itself" into the "for us."If a perceived object were denied its worldliness, then it would seemingly be impossible for it to retain its identity, and hence objectivity, through multiple modes of experience. I could not come back to the same room, the same chair, the same desk, the same piece of paper, and so on, if they were not worldly beings. For in numerically distinct, temporally differentiated experiences I nonetheless "have" the same objects. While they are given in individual experiences, and hence are "for me," they simultaneously transcend those experiences in that the same, self-identical object can be returned to again, and again, and again. This independence from consciousness, however, does not establish such entities as absolute *concreta*, but points to their essential dependence on the world, for their very independence from consciousness.

What Husserl's transcendental phenomenology attempts, however, is the replacement of the world as absolute *concretum*, with transcendental subjectivity. Via the *epoche*, the belief in the existence of the pre-given world is put out of play. If the world is indeed the final foundation, that which is first in itself, that more comprehensive unity with which all else is necessarily linked as *momenta* of the original whole, then such a suspension should produce a total slipping away of all objectivity. Through it we should, in Nietzsche's words, "feel the breath of empty space"[53] accompanying the "death" of the final ground. An annihilation of the world should be the annihilation of all Being, in the same way that the elimination of visual extension annihilates the Being of color. But the anticipated collapse into nothingness does not occur. Instead, a phenomenological residuum remains as the domain of pure consciousness. Objects and their horizons are not eliminated, but reemerge as correlates of acts which do in fact achieve the transcendence which was previously, naively, attributed to the world.

In the fifth and sixth Investigations of the *Logical Investigations*, Husserl came to recognize that the objectivity and self-identity of ideal objects could be attained precisely through an analysis of their appearance to consciousness. In such fashion, we witness the birth of objectivity. In opposition to any psychologistic interpretation of this, Husserl claims:

There is an original evidence that, in repeated acts, which are quite alike or else similar, the produced judgments, arguments, and so forth, are not merely quite alike or similar, but numerically, identically the same judgments, arguments, and the like. Their making an appearance in the domain of consciousness is multiple. The particular, formative processes of thinking are temporally outside one another (viewed as real psychic processes in real human beings, they are outside one another in objective time); they are individually different and separated. Not so, however, the thoughts that are thought in the thinking.[54]

This capacity of consciousness for ojectivization (constitution), when universalized, leads to a fully actualized transcendental idealism.[55] Consciousness, when purified of all worldly interpretations, embraces both the "for us" and the "in itself" as *momenta* of the one, only, concrete whole: transcendental subjectivity.

The logic of wholes and parts, therefore, has led us along a path from individual entities and their pieces to the world, and finally to transcendental subjectivity, as that more comprehensive whole upon which all else is founded. That which is independent is "in and for itself," while the dependent *momenta* "can only have being-in."[56] The return to origins in Husserl's thought, hence, is a return to the absolute *concreta* of transcendental consciousness,

> in which all other regions of Being have their root, to which they are essentially related, on which they are one and all *dependent* in an *essential* way.[57]

MOTIVES FOR THE TRANSCENDENTAL TURN

If we take this line of interpretation, and then ask for the motivation underlying the transcendental turn in Husserl's thought, we find that the ready response of the quest for apodicticity is insufficient. Apodicticity, as we saw in the last chapter, is indeed a component of the ideal of science. But apodicticity is not attained with the transcendental reduction, as transcendental. A critique of transcendental experience, an "apodictic reduction," is necessary to overcome the naivete of the transcendental character of phenomenology. We cannot, therefore, situate the significance of the transcendental turn within an interpretive horizon which explicates it in terms of the ideal of apodictic evidence.

What we have seen is that the concept of evidence elicited from a noematic analysis of scientific striving also entails the notion of a hierarchy, progressing toward that which is first in itself, that is, toward that which is founding and not in turn founded. The *Logical Investigations* have provided an insight into the meaning of this idea of "firstness" as foundation, via the logic of wholes and parts. The philosophical significance of this logic, in conjunction with the "principle of all principles" which, for Husserl, situates rationality in a rigorous allegiance to intuitive givenness, is the claim that reason itself, as eidetic rationality, demands the transcendental turn. Only in this way can "an essential transcendental illusion"[58] be overcome.

There is no finite, world-immanent problematic which could ever elicit the denial of the world entailed in the transcendental reduction. But this does not necessarily imply the total lack of all motivations for transcendental phenomenology. The decision to become a philosopher, to live under and toward the ideal of rationality, is

the idea of a resolve of the will to shape one's whole personal life into the synthetic unity of a life of universal self-responsibility and, correlatively, to shape oneself into the true "I," the free autonomous "I" which seeks to realize his innate reason, the striving to be true to himself, to be able to remain identical with himself as a reasonable "I."[59]

Let us recall that which is formulated as the "principle of all principles" in *Ideas I*, and presented as a "first methodological principle" in the *Cartesian Meditations*:

that every primordial dator (*gebende*) intuition is a source of authority for knowledge, that whatever presents itself in intuition in primordial form (as it were in its bodily reality) is simply to be accepted as it gives itself out to be, though only within the limits in which it then presents itself.[60]

The logic of wholes and parts, as a formal, a priori theory of objects, has given us an insight into the idea of objects which are essentially fragmentary or incomplete, which always point beyond themselves to a more comprehensive whole. When such objects give themselves to an intuitive, rational consciousness, this pointing beyond on the part of the objects is evident. *Momenta* or dependent objects give themselves bodily, but only within certain limits, as parts of some whole.

The movement toward transcendental consciousness, therefore, can be seen as the continual progression of reason, guided by the principle of intuition, from part to whole, which in turn is seen as a part, to a whole, and so forth. We must see both that which gives itself, *and its limits*. To see its limits, however, is to see it as partial or fragmentary, that is, as a moment of a larger whole. That whole, in turn, may give itself, but also with limits. The continual recognition of the limits of givenness testifies to the essentially partial nature of the objectivity in question, as well as to the openness to the whole on the part of the philosopher. In general, the development traced in these pages has been from the particular object, to the world, to transcendental consciousness, as the final and only absolute *concretum*.

The transcendental turn, then, is nothing other than the vehicle of eidetic rationality itself. It cannot be authentically interpreted as a contraction of subjectivity upon itself, a contraction to a single point, to a fragment or part. "Subjectivism can only be overcome by the most all-embracing and consistent subjectivism (the transcendental.")[61] Infinite domains of significance need not be renounced in the name of certitude.

The transcendental reduction brings into view for the first time the absolute character of subjectivity, but not as the sole instance of an apodictic evidence (and hence as the only legitimate theme for philosophical science). Instead, the absolute of subjectivity is that of "firstness" as foundational, as that unity upon which all else is dependent. It is transcendental subjectivity in its full concretion, as *ego-cogito-cogitatum*; not as a pure form of unity conceived in abstraction from phenomenal reality. Husserl's phenomenology thus claims to be the science of the whole, of the original sphere of Being, that is, "all-embracing ontology as first philosophy."[62] It reawakens philosophy to the task of wholistic comprehension.

If we conceive of intuitive reason moving within the medium of parts and wholes, and tending toward completeness, then we recognize that the transcendental domain of consciousness does not ultimately designate a separate region of Being, so much as the interpretive horizon proper for philosophical science. What distinguishes pure phenomenological psychology, for example, from transcendental phenomenological philosophy, is not an ontic difference between the psychological ego and the transcendental ego. The two egos are not two, but one, only viewed from a difference perspective or attitude. There is no distinct noumenal self nor absolute "I" that stands apart from the natural, worldly self, separated, as it were, by some sort of veil.[63]

It is just this field of transcendental self-experience (conceived in full concreteness) which in every case can, *through mere alteration of attitude*, be changed into psychological self-experience. In this transition, an identity of the I is necessarily brought about.[64]

What distinguishes the "two" egos is the context or horizon within which they are seen and interpreted, or the whole of which they are parts. When the ego is seen as worldly, then the horizon for its interpretation, the whole to which it belongs, is the world. When seen as transcendental, there is no external horizon, for there is no whole or more comprehensive unity upon which it depends. It has only the *infinite, inner* horizon of temporality.[65] It is in this sense that the transcendental ego is a pure "in itself," as related only to itself. This enclosure of subjectivity upon itself, however, does not preclude relation to the world; rather, it constitutes it. The world first comes to be as the necessary correlate of such consciousness.

Ultimately, if the transcendental is the domain of true beginnings, it is not due to its apodicticity, but to its giving us that which is first, as the original whole. All other beginnings are abstract, in the sense that they mistake a part for the whole or fail even to consider the question. Such an abstract character is necessary for partial sciences, both a priori and a posteriori, which study parts or regions of Being. But if universal science begins abstractly, it condemns itself as internally inconsistent.

The problem of beginnings then, in Husserl, can be called a contextual problem to the degree that what is in question is the context or framework within which philosophical self-reflection can actualize itself. This is made eminently clear in the *Crisis*, where Husserl notes that "the point is not to secure objectivity but to understand it."[66] Our worldly experience of objects is secured on its own terms, in and through other worldly experiences. The objectivity of my empirical claims can be enhanced only through further sense experiences. But an understanding of the objectivity of the objects of those experiences is presupposed by the natural attitutde. Philosophical reflection, according to Husserl, uncovers transcendental subjectivity and its constitutive achievements to be the *foundation* of that objectivity. But it is not an epistemologically securing foundation. Husserl's transcendental phenomenology attempts to reawaken us from a naive (partial) enthrallment in pregiven objects, to an insight into their essential dependence upon the life of consciousness. Only from such a perspective, only against such a background, can their objectivity be understood.

The interpretation of the transcendental reduction presented here is itself, of course, only formal. The concrete way in which the relationship between the independent and the dependent is explicated in transcendental terms is via the concept of constitution. The uniquely constitutive character of this relation accounts for the "transcendence within immanence" achieved via transcendental subjectivity. Nonetheless, this interpretation sketches out the basic, formal structure, or formal logic, of the transcendental turn. Any material explications of Husserl's thought must be consistent with these results in the same way that all material ontologies must be governed by the laws of formal ontology.

In addition, it should be noted that the application of a pretranscendental theory of objects as an interpretive framework for the explication of the movement to transcendental consciousness, such as has been attempted here, does not imply that the results obtained correspond with Husserl's explicit intentions, nor that they constitute a logically coherent philosophical *system*. Husserl nowhere presents or introduces the transcendental reduction in just these terms. But the ideal of correspondence with authorial intention is not the interpretive norm animating these reflections. What we have attempted is the discovery of an inner rationale, in terms of an autonomous *philosophical* problematic, which could serve as the implicit teleological impetus for the development of Husserl's thinking. What is the question to which transcendental phenomenology claims to offer an answer? Along with Fink, we agree that is the question "concerning the origin of the world."[67] How this question comes to be formulated, and the meaning that it has for Husserl, is what the previous pages have attempted to unfold.

Two general conclusions can be drawn from the preceding material. First, it points to a fundamental continuity in the development of Husserl's phenomenology throughout all of its stages. Any revolutions in phenomenology, such as the transcendental turn introduced in 1907, can be comprehended as consistent with, and demanded by, the "logic of phenomenology." If one defines phenomenology as a descriptive, eidetic science, proceeding in light of intuition, and if one conceives the objects of intuition along the formal lines of wholes and parts, and philosophically seeks the most wholistic comprehension possible, then the result is a *transcendental* phenomenology. Husserl's idealism, thus, is not a turn away from the true principles of phenomenology, but is the product of the courageous and radical pursuit of "the things themselves," along strictly phenomenological lines.

A second consequence of this interpretation is that if transcendental subjectivity is the final *concretum* or original whole, then all intelligible questions must, *in principle* at any rate, find their solution within the transcendental domain. As Husserl specifically states, "in phenomenology, all rational problems have their place. . . ."[68] Any question which cannot, in principle, be meaningfully answered from the perspective of transcendental phenomenology must be either a meaningless question, or must point to a limitation to transcendental subjectivity. The suggestion of essential limits to transcendental reflection points, in turn, to its "momentary" character.

It is on this note that we shall undertake the transition to Heidegger's conception of phenomenology in relation to the question of Being. To what extent does Husserl's thought come to terms with the *Seinsfrage* in Heidegger's sense? To what extent does it even allow it to arise? If this question escapes transcendental, constitutive analyses, is it because it is basically an unintelligible question? Or does Heidegger's philosophy point to an inherent weakness in transcendental phenomenology? Does it disclose an essential incompleteness or fragmentary character which undermines its status as radical philosophical science?

4
Transcendental Subjectivity and Being-in-the-World

THE PRECEDING CHAPTER, through its attempt at a unified interpretation of the transcendental reduction, brought into view the central themes of the principle of all principles in correlation with the logic of wholes and parts. Husserl's absolute allegiance to the principle of intuitive givenness, though always within the limits of that givenness, can be viewed as an explication of the basic phenomenological maxim: "To the things themselves." To talk about that which is given within the limits of its givenness is to talk about a part being given with a broader context or horizon, recognizing the latter as the whole to which the part belongs. In this vein, for example, Sokolowski notes that the *epoche* is Husserl's device which prevents sciences of parts of the world, such as psychologism, mechanism, or the mathematization of nature and man, from ruling over the whole.[1] *N.S.*

This "logic of the transcendental reduction" makes intelligible both the inversion of the meaning of Being found in *Ideas I*, and the transcendental idealism of the *Cartesian Meditations*, and does so in terms of an inversion of the whole-part relationship. We have seen that what distinguishes the natural and the philosophical (transcendental) attitudes is that which each attitude takes to be the original whole. The essence of the natural attitude lies in the belief in the existence of the pregiven world (*Weltdoxa*). This is the ultimate horizon within which we encounter all the different types of entities which populate the various regions of Being. These entities may be encountered in a scientific or prescientific manner, but in either event the world still functions as the horizon for their encounter. The ordinary act of reflection which brings about explicit self-consciousness in no way alters the functioning of this world-horizon, for the

"transcendence within immanence"
of. incarnation.
80   The Question of a Phenomenological Beginning

self so grasped is still a worldly self, a psychological or anthropological ego.

The transcendental reduction, however, inverts this whole-part relationship, so that after its performance, the ultimate horizon is subjectivity or consciousness. The world is now seen as belonging to consciousness in a unique and peculiar sense, in a transcendental sense. Consciousness, Husserl claims, is able to achieve a transcendence within immanence, so that all the objects of the world, while being *essentially dependent* (*momenta*) on consciousness for their meaning and their Being *(Sinn und Sein)*, nonetheless maintain their full objectivity and identity in transcending the particular multiplicity of acts through which they are given. Consciousness is now seen as containing both the "in itself" and the "for us," so that the objectivity of the objects which the natural attitude attributes to the world is now achieved by subjectivity, as transcendental, world-constituting subjectivity. Hence, this transcendence within immanence can be seen as the Husserlian attempt to overcome Cartesian dualism.

The studies which are carried out within the transcendental reduction are intentional analyses. The object or theme of transcendental reflection is ontically identical with that of pure psychological reflection, namely, consciousness, whose essence lies in intentionality. Depending on the types of questions governing the particular phenomenological analyses, these studies may be oriented primarily toward the noetic or noematic components of intentional life. But the essential correlation between *poesis* and *noema* is always maintained. Thus *Ideas I* characterizes intentionality as "the main theme of phenomenology,"[2] and this assertion is reaffirmed throughout all of Husserl's writings. Intentionality, as the essence of consciousness, is continually established as the groundwork upon which all subsequent studies and analyses are undertaken.

With the theme of intentionality, therefore, we have a way of making concrete the results of our previous interpretation of the transcendental reduction. How is it that intentional analyses carried out within the framework of the transcendental reduction differ from those concrete analyses which, while being eidetic and phenomenological, still persist within the world-horizon? This is merely another way of asking about the distinction between phenomenological psychology, which, according to Husserl, utilizes the phenomenological and eidetic reductions, and transcendental phenomenology, which "adds" the transcendental reduction. We know, formally speaking, that what distinguishes the two is the ultimate horizon within

"Intentionality" = The essence of consciousness. = groundwork

which they are effected. But with regard to content itself, what does this distinction mean?

The way in which we shall ask this question will be as follows. The eidetic reduction will be presupposed. This is not to say that it may not contain within itself a variety of problems, but only that for our purposes here it will be taken for granted as an acceptable methodological device for pure psychology and philosophy. Their concern is with the essential structures of the phenomena, and not with the particularizing details of the instances studied. We shall, however, attend more closely to the phenomenological reduction, that movement of thought which gives us the phenomena, that is, the subjective processes through which we become "conscious of" all different types of objects.[3] This discovery of psychic life as essentially being "consciousness of" is nothing other than intentionality itself, at least conceived in its most general and indeterminate form. Our main question then is, how does the tanscendental reduction alter our understanding of intentionality so as to transform it from a psychological characteristic of psychic beings into a philosophical concept of the highest significance?

Approaching the question in this manner will serve two main purposes. First, it will fill in the details of our previous interpretation of the transcendental reduction, which was only sketched out formally, by showing the way in which the issue of the whole-part relationship, transcendental subjectivity versus the world, bears on our ultimate self-understanding. What does it mean to pursue the Socratic dictum, "Know thyself," in terms of our intentional comportment toward the real? Second, the issue of intentionality will be used as a bridge to Heidegger's phenomenology. We shall look to certain passages in Heidegger's thought as articulated in the period from 1927 to 1929 in which he explicitly or implicitly poses the *Seinsfrage* in terms of intentionality. Our basic claim in this regard will be that both Husserl and Heidegger go beyond intentionality in a certain sense, although the ways in which they do so are radically different. Neither thinker aims at negating or devaluing the concept, but instead attempts to provide the context, horizon, or whole, within which intentionality can be grasped as it is "in itself."

INTENTIONALITY

The concept of intentionality as the distinguishing characteristic of consciousness was first put forth by the Nineteenth Century psy-

chologist and philosopher Franz Brentano. One of Brentano's primary
concerns was to secure a scientific basis for experimental psychology
by grounding it on a more radical "empirical" basis than had been
previously done.[4] The nature of this empirical basis is left somewhat
ambiguous by Brentano, in that it allows room, for example, for a
type of ideal intuition (*ideale Anschauung*), though what this might
mean and how it is possible remain indeterminate. But what is
involved in his approach is a new, descriptive psychology, one which
would provide the basis for a genetic psychology. The primary task
of such a descriptive discipline would be the precise determination
of what belongs to a psychological phenomenon as such, differentiating it from the realm of physical phenomena.

In this vein, Brentano saw that psychology, as an autonomous
scientific discipline, could not justifiably orient itself toward physics
and the physical sciences.[5] And for Brentano, what distinguished a
psychological from a nonpsychological phenomenon was the former's
intentionality. What Brentano meant by the intentionality of the
psychological phenomena was that they contained within themselves
a "reference to an object."[6] In what sense the psychic act *refers* to
an object, and how the object of this referring is to be understood,
are central problems not only for psychology, but for philosophy as
well. They are the noetic and noematic components of intentional
analysis. We need not concern ourselves here with the manner in
which Brentano approached this problem, for our main concern now
is with Husserl's conception of phenomenological psychology. And
from his perspective, despite the seminal nature of Brentano's thinking, it never entered the genuine domain of phenomenological psychology.[7]

Consciousness, in its essence, is intentional. How is this to be
understood? The usual account of intentionality suggests that its basic
meaning resides in the notion that "without exception, every conscious process is, in itself, a consciousness *of* such and such. . . ."[8]
Eidetic reflection upon consciousness, therefore aims at

> the essential nature of "the consciousness of something," fol-
> lowing for instance, our consciousness of the existence of material
> things, living bodies and men, or that of technical and literary
> works, and so forth.[9]

The first point to be noted, then, is that consciousness so conceived
does not consist of a bundle of data, of ultimately simple "things"

(impressions) which can be combined, for example, according to laws of association. Consciousness is a process or activity. Intentionality does not belong to the ego or psyche as a property of a substance which can relate itself to objects, but which, in its purity, first exists as an identical substrate or as a multiplicity of such identical things.[10] Instead, consciousness contains *within itself* this relationship:

> the manifold cogitations, relating to what is worldly, bear this relationship *within themselves* [Italics mine] . . . . Each *cogito*, each conscious process, . . . "means" something or other, and bears in itself, in this manner peculiar to the meant, its particular *cogitatum*.[11]

This, of course, is a very enigmatic claim. If we identify the real with that which exists substantially, as a self-enclosed, self-identical thing which can have certain properties, then to say that consciousness *is* intentional, rather than it *has* intentionality as a property, seems nonsensical. It appears to stand outside the basic categories which render beings intelligible. The intentionality of consciousness is what makes these processes "phenomena" in the Husserlian sense, and is clearly directed against any reification of consciousness. Consciousness is real, although it is not a *res*. This means that consciousness is also not a nonextended *res*, a thinking *res*. It is not a thing at all; "it" is not a substance. So, for example, if one were to accept the Cartesian identification of the Being of nature with extension, then the elimination of extension is the elimination of the Being of nature. In the same way, for phenomenology, the elimination of the intentionality of consciousness would result in the nonbeing of consciousness.[12]

This manner of explicating the concept of intentionality, as directed against the reification of consciousness, is treated in depth in Husserl's "Philosophy as Rigorous Science" (1910–11). While this article was published prior to *Ideas I*, it still is later than the initial transcendental turn of the *The Idea of Phenomenology* (1907). In advocating the ideals of scientific philosophy, Husserl argues against both naturalism and historicism. Husserl sees naturalistic philosophy as claiming that,

> whatever *is* is either itself physical, belonging to the unified totality of physical nature, or it is in fact psychical, but then merely a variable dependent on the physical, at best a secondary, "parallel accompaniment."[13]

This interpretation of the *ontos on*, the "really real", leads to the naturalizing of consciousness, as well as of the ideals and norms of axiology, practical philosophy, and logic. Because psychology has borrowed its most fundamental concepts from the sciences of nature rather than from the "phenomena themselves," Husserl views it as being at a stage analogous to that of pre-Galilean physics.[14] Psychology can become an exact, experimental science only insofar as its a priori is worked out in advance. The mere refinement or multiplication of experimental techniques alone will not enhance its scientific character, so long as psychology "has not considered what lies in the 'sense' of psychological experience and what 'demands' being (in the sense of the psychical) of itself makes on method."[15]

It is in this regard that Husserl sees the discovery of intentionality by Brentano, and its investigation by Stumpf and Lipps, for example, as the development of "a truly epoch making impulse."[16] Husserl views this as "epoch making" in a manner reminiscent of Galileo, in that the a priori of Nature which made possible modern mathematical physics is now to be complemented by a phenomenological a priori of consciousness.

A phenomenological pure psychology is absolutely necessary as the foundation for the building up of an "exact" empirical psychology, which since its modern beginnings has been sought according to the model of the exact pure sciences of physical nature.[17]

And the methodological device which makes accesible this material a priori (regional ontology) is the phenomenological reduction.

This "naturalism," against which the phenomenological reduction is directed, can infiltrate our understanding of intentionality, unless we exercise the utmost effort to attend to the things themselves. In the *Logical Investigations*, a work which, despite certain errors, nonetheless attains to the level of a pure, descriptive phenomenology, Husserl explicitly combats two "natural" misinterpretations of intentionality:

First, that we are dealing with a real (*realen*) event or a real (*reales*) relationship, taking place between "consciousness" or "the ego," on the one hand, and the thing of which there is consciousness, on the other; secondly, that we are dealing with a relation between two things, both present in equally real (*reell*)

noema = intentional object

fashion in consciousness, an act and an intentional object, or with a sort of box-within-box structure of mental contents.[18]

The latter point has certain scholastic overtones to it, assuming that the intentional object has a kind of "mental in-existence" such as an image, representation, or intelligible species within consciousness. The intentional object for Husserl is not an immanent component of the stream of consciousness, as are, for example, the sensile-hyle and intentional-morphe. The *intentional object* or *noema* exists "intentionality"; that is, it is the intended sense as such. In perception, it is the "perceived as such"; in desire, the "desired as such"; in fear, the "feared as such." These noemata belong to the "sphere of sense."[19]

> The unreality of entities belonging to this sphere lies . . . in a certain independence of the concrete act by which they are actualized, in the sense that every one of them may correspond, as identically the same, to another act, and even to an indefinite number of acts.[20]

Husserl emphasizes this "unreality" or "irreal" nature of the intentional object in the *Logical Investigations*.

> The "immanent," "mental object" is not therefore part of the descriptive or real make-up (*descriptiven reellen Bestand*) of the experience, it is in truth not really immanent or mental. But it also does not exist extramentally, it does not exist at all.[21]

The transcendence within immance of the *noema*, therefore, does not refer to a relation between two things either; the other possible misinterpretation previously mentioned. By saying it "does not exist at all," Husserl clearly means that it is neither a physical thing, nor a *reell* component of psychic being.

If these prejudices can be overcome, then from Husserl's perspective, a pure phenomenological psychology is possible. Intentionality can be understood on its own terms, and studied in all its multiple modes, types, and levels.

> For psychology, the universal task presents itself: to investigate systematically the elementary intentionalities and from out of these unfold the typical forms of intentional processes, their

possible variants, their syntheses to new forms, their structural composition, and from this advance towards a descriptive knowledge of the totality of mental processes, towards a comprehensive type of the life of the psychic.[22]

Once again this is possible only on the basis of a proper grasp of the intentional directedness of *cogitatio* (*noesis*) toward *cogitatum* (*noema*), toward the meant as such in the particular mode of the act meaning it. Thus Husserl sees in the *Logical Investigations* the initial realization of Brentano's demand for a psychology of intentionality.

What is new in the *Logical Ivestigations* is found not at all in the merely ontological investigations, which had a one-sided influence contrary to the innermost sense of the work, but rather in the subjectively directed investigations (above all the Fifth and Sixth, in the Second Volume of 1901) in which, for the first time, the *cogitata qua cogitata*, as essential moments of each conscious experience as it is given in genuine inner experience, come into their own and immediately come to dominate the whole method of intentional analysis.[23]

The grasping of *cogitata as cogitata* frees consciousness, and hence intentionality, from the naturalizing tendencies toward reification under which all previous analyses have labored. Consciousness is now seen as *achieving* a certain objectivity in that the intended sense "transcends" the particular acts in which it is meant. It does so by maintaining an identity throughout the manifold modes of its being intended.

With the above descriptions we have covered one of the two characteristics of the phenomenological reduction which Husserl mentions in the *Encyclopaedia Britannica* article, namely:

the methodically practiced seizing and describing of the multiple "appearances" as appearances of their unitary objects and their unities as unities of components of meaning accuring to them each time in their appearance.[24]

The other aspect of the phenomenological reduction

consists in the methodical and rigorously consistent *epoche* of every objective positing in the psychic sphere, both of the individual phenomenon and of the whole psychic field in general.[25]

This is the bracketing of the objective world taken simply as existing, and its replacement with the world "as meant" in consciousness. This psychological *epoche*, however, is taken to be an abstraction, a narrowing down of our vision to a particular part of the world. It is, as Husserl says in the *Cartesian Meditations*, "the abstractive restricting of anthropological research to purely psychic life."[26] The world as meant belongs to this subjective sphere, but in abstraction from the world as it is in itself.

As we have seen, the transcendental reduction, in contrast, is not characterized by its abstracting from any wholistic framework; but rather precisely by its discovery of the absolute *concretum* or whole. The transcendental problem, for Husserl, is determining by its "all-inclusiveness."[27] It is generated out of the enigmatic confrontation between the world as meant and the world as it is in itself. The world as meant has been seen to belong to psychological subjectivity, in the form of the noematic correlate. The enigma is how consciousness, the subjectivity here considered,

> manages in its immanence, that something which mainfests itself can present itself as something existing in itself, and not only as something meant, but as something authenticated in concordant experience.[28]

In other words, how does meaning or sense disclose, or relate to, an existing being as it is in itself?

What is crucial for the differentiation between the transcendental and the psychological is the recognition that the "it" which "manages" this alleged achievement, prior to the transcendental reduction, is taken as a human subject in the world. This psyche is always the psyche of animal realities, of natural, worldly beings. Even when grasped in its purity, in its genuine intentionality properly understood, the horizon within which this grasping occurs remains the universal, human, world-horizon. An abstraction from the world leaves the world untouched as an interpretive horizon. The problematic thus formulated remains totally enmeshed within a dualism, and *the traditional epistemological problem of transcendence remains essentially the same.*[29]

What the transcendental reduction realizes is that that horizon within which the subject becomes thematically aware of itself, and from which the problem of transcendence is posed, is in turn itself the noematic achievement of that same subjetivity. Consciousness is both "in" the world and "of" the world. The recognition of the source or origin of that horizon allows us to neutralize it, so that we can witness its genesis rather than presuppose its universal validity. We thus must speak of a new or deeper subjectivity, or perhaps better,

of a certain subject doubling. From the perspective of psychology human beings are psycho-physical subjects of a psychic life in the world. From the transcendental perspective men are subjects of a transcendental and world-constituting life.[30]

At this transcendental level, "it follows *eo ipso* that nothing human is to be found, neither soul nor psychic life nor real psychophysical human beings; all this belongs to the phenomenon, to the world as constituted pole."[31]

The transcendental phenomenology of Husserl, therefore, can be described as the attempt to comprehend the "origin of the world,"[32] how the world comes to stand as world, or the Being of the world. The noematic sense is not something which stands in between subjectivity and real things, which mediates between an existent subject and an existent object. It is not something which "stands between" as do the Kantian forms of intuition and understanding; which, while making phenomena accessible, bar our access to "things in themselves." The sense of the "in itself," of independent existence, emerges in the intentional syntheses of conscious life. The "for us" is that which is affectively given and comes to be given in the development of intentional experience. But that which is so given always emerges within a horizon of the merely intended, which can be fulfilled or cancelled through a synthetic conversion into the affectively apprehended.

Only an uncovering of the horizon of experience ultimately clarifies the "actuality" and "transcendency" of the world, at the same time showing the world to be inseparable from transcendental subjectivity, which constitutes actuality of being and sense. The reference to harmonious infinities of further possible experience, starting from each world-experience, where "actually existing object" can have sense only as a unity meant and meanable in the nexus of consciousness, a unity that would be given as itself in a perfect experiential evidence—manifestly signifies that an actual object belonging to a world or, all the more so, a world itself, is an infinite idea, related to infinities of harmonious combinable experiences—an idea that is the correlate of the idea of a perfectly experiential evidence, a complete synthesis of possible experience.[33]

And Husserl goes on to say that this Idea in the Kantian sense, this

actually existing object indicates a particular system within this multiplicity, the system of evidences relating to the object and belonging together in such a manner that they combine to make up one (though perhaps an infinite) total evidence.[34]

The Being of entities, understood as existence or *Vorhandenheit*, is situated in their presence to consciousness. The consciousness to which they are present is transcendental consciousness, and so understood, it is the ultimate sphere of origins. The transcendental reduction, therefore, provides the context within which intentionality can accomplish that which it claims to accomplish, namely, a presence to beings in themselves. The reversion to consciousness, therefore, in Husserl's phenomenology, the bracketing of Being, is undertaken in order ultimately to clarify the meaning of the Being of entities. And this ontological onset, once more, must be clearly differentiated from the material and formal ontologies which can function outside the sphere of transcendental analysis. As objectively oriented, they fail to uncover the most primordial sense of the Being of entities, always operating within the implicit realism of the natural attitude. For they say nothing about the "actually existing object" as actually existing, nothing about "being qua being," but only develop the essential predicates belonging to the object presupposing its Being to be that of a worldly object.

THE "SUBJECTIVE" TURN IN HUSSERL AND HEIDEGGER

We have now arrived at that point in our understanding of the innermost essence of the transcendental phenomenology of Husserl where it will be possible to make a meaningful comparison with the problematic of Heidegger as first formulated in the period from 1927 to 1929. In what manner can our interpretation serve to illuminate the relationship between the phenomenologies of Husserl and Heidegger, both in terms of similarities and differences? It is often thought that the common ground between the two is so narrow that any account which honestly comes to terms with the genuine substance of their positions, rather than with the early historical ties between the two, will find only radical difference. It is a commonplace triviality to note that Heidegger rejects the transcendental reduction in his phenomenological-ontological treatise *Being and Time*. In opposition to the bracketing of Being we find the question of the meaning of Being. In opposition to a worldless transcendental subjectivity, we find the "subject" as Being-in-the-World; and in such a radical and essential sense that now the terms "subject," "ego," "consciousness," and so forth are no longer philosophically useful.

Given this type of radical divergence, how can one seriously speak about any ground of continuity between Husserl and Heidegger? But with regard to the first point mentioned above, the bracketing of Being, we have now established that this movement is undertaken in the service of the problem of Being. We shall see that the way in which Husserl and Heidegger conceive of Being, is very different. Nonetheless, the Being of entities is still that which determines them as entities, just insofar as they "are." Our interpretation of the transcendental reduction, which subordinated the epistemological problematic of a beginning point which would be apodictic to the ontological problem of a foundational beginning securing that which entities depend upon for their Being, makes it possible to say that when Heidegger asks the "Being-question" (*Seinsfrage*), he not only remains within *the* traditional question of philosophy, but also moves within the Husserlian dynamic of phenomenology as well.

We can cite explicit evidence for this in Heidegger's revisions to Husserl's first draft of the *Encyclopaedia Britannica* article: "Attempt at a Second Revision. Introduction. The Idea of Phenomenology and the Regression to Consciousness."[35] In these pages Heidegger works with a Husserlian text and formulates the problem of Being in terms of a return to consciousness, and more particularly to transcendental subjectivity. Heidegger first makes some very general remarks on the relationship between the problem of Being, on the one hand, and thought, *logos* and consciousness, on the other, moving historically from Parmenides to Kant. He then asks:

Is this shift in perspective from beings to consciousness aribtrary or is it perhaps demanded by the peculiarity of that which, under the title of Being, is constantly attended to as the problem area of philosophy? The clarification in principle of the necessity for regression to conscious awareness, the radical and explicit determination of the way or path of the procedural steps of this retrogression, the fundamental circumscription and systematic exploration of the sphere of pure subjectivity which is opened up along this way back: such is what constitutes phenomenology.[36]

He goes on to say that this subjectivity cannot be a psychological one, even a "pure" psychological one.

Because in this subjectivity the Being of all that which for the subject can be experienced in a different way, the transcendent in the broadest sense, is constituted, it is called transcendental subjectivity.[37]

It is clear that this formulation and understanding of phenomenology should not be identified with Heidegger's own comprehension of phenomenology. The latter must be sought in *Being and Time*, as well as in *The Essence of Reasons*, where Heidegger explicitly and implicitly develops the *Seinsfrage* in terms of phenomenology. Instead, it is best seen as Heidegger's interpretation of Husserl's phenomenology and of its significance. The talk of "pure subjectivity," and of the "constitution" of Being in and by this subjectivity do not appear in Heidegger's own works; works which reveal a fundamental opposition to such concepts. But Heidegger still undertakes the "subjective turn" in his own way, so that the pecularity of the relationship between Being and "consciousness"[38] is still manifest.

Of course it could be objected that Heidegger's introduction nowhere appears in Husserl's own version of the article which was finally published. If this is Heidegger's interpretation of Husserl's phenomenology, then Husserl's own rejection of it seems to warrant the dismissal of this interpretation, at least as corresponding to Husserl's own intentions. In this vein, Spiegelberg suggests that it is Heidegger's characterization of the goal of philosophy as concerned with Being that Husserl found most objectionable.[39] It surely seems that Husserl could not have objected to Heidegger's presentation of the transcendental, for it corresponds very closely to Husserl's as found in the *Cartesian Meditations*.[40]

But what does seem objectionable to Husserl is presenting the transcendental in an introduction, rather than gradually being led to it via a consideration of phenomenological psychology. As far as the ontological characterization is concerned, it too reappears in Husserl's own version as soon as the transcendental dimension is introduced. With Part III of the article, we reach the transcendental, and Section A is entitled "Transcendental Phenomenology as Ontology." There phenomenology is described as the science

of the totality of objectively existing beings, and certainly not in an attitude of natural positivity; rather, in the full concretion of that being in general which derives its sense of being and its validity from the correlative intentional constitution. . . . Accordingly, a phenomenology properly carried through is the truly universal ontology as over against the only illusory all-embracing ontology in positivity. . . .[41]

As has been mentioned, and will be developed in the following pages, the manner in which Husserl and Heidegger understand Being, as that which determines entities as entities, differs radically. But their common concern with Being is what makes possible this difference.

Thus there remains a variety of possibilities for understanding Husserl's failure to include Heidegger's introduction in the final version, other than claiming that Heidegger's interpretation presented there is simply wrong. References to the transcendental and to ontology may have no place in such an opening statement from Husserl's perspective, in that at that level they remain so saturated with naturalistic prejudices that they could only be misunderstood. Also, Heidegger's references to the history of philosophy as precedent carry no weight in Husserl's eyes. While Husserl later attempts to situate his own phenomenology within a historical perspective, he does not do so by appealing to historical facts as Heidegger seems to in his introduction.

But if we have overcome this initial polarity between Husserl and Heidegger in recognizing that the former does not surrender the ontological question in the name of epistemic certitude, there still remains the issue of the transcendental reduction, although the problem now receives a different, and proper, formulation. Our inquiry is now directed to the adequacy of this reduction to the task that it sets itself. Can transcendental phenomenology serve as "the truly universal ontology"? Does the transcendental reduction give us the absolute *concretum*, that final whole upon which all else essentially depends? Heidegger's answer is that it does not. From a Heideggerian perspective, the transcendental reduction fails to illuminate its own presuppositions. Despite the fact that it aims at the meaning of the Being of entities, it always works within an implicit understanding of Being. And this understanding of Being is one in which the genuine ontological dimension gets closed off. For Heidegger, the presuppositions of the transcendental reduction cancel its significance. We shall now attempt to examine this problem in some detail.

While we previously suggested that Husserl's objections to Heidegger's introductory paragraphs of the proposed *Encyclopaedia Britannica* article may not deal so much with the basic substance as with its mode of presentation, it was also noted that this understanding of phenomenology should not be identified with that of Heidegger. In Heidegger's phenomenology, both in *Being and Time* and *The Essence of Reasons*, we find no transcendental reduction, no transcendental subjectivity in the Husserlian sense, and correlatively, no analyses of the constitution of beings. *Letter to Roman Ingarden 1927*

Husserl recognizes these omissions in Heidegger's version of phenomenology and criticizes it accordingly. In a letter to Roman Ingarden in December of 1927, he says, "Heidegger has not grasped the whole meaning of the phenomenological reduction."[42] And in the marginal notes to his copy of *Being and Time*, Husserl says the following:

> Heidegger transposes or translates the constitutive, phenomenological clarification of beings . . . the total region of the world, into anthropology. The entire problematic is transferred. For the ego, he writes Dasein, and so forth. Thus, all its deeper sense becomes unclear and it loses its philosophical worth.
> What is said there is my own teaching, only without its deeper foundation. This is, in my view, the way to an intentional psychology of the personality of the personal lifeworld. . . .[43]

And with regard to constitution, he says in two other passages: "This does not present constitutive phenomenology" and, "Why is there no constitutive phenomenology?"[44] With Heidegger's failure to implement the transcendental reduction, the constitutive dimension is

H transcendentali an a relapse to psychologism

also eliminated, at least with regard to objects.[45] From Husserl's perspective this implies that it is no longer the world that is constituted, but rather only *meanings* within a subject in the world.

Of course Heidegger is not the only phenomenologist to renounce the transcendental turn. The realists of the Göttingen and Munich schools also rejected this aspect of Husserl, seeing in it a relapse into the subjectivism (psychologism) which the *Logical Investigations* had successfully overcome.[46] For these thinkers, the *Logical Investigations* proved most valuable in the development of the method of essential intuition, and in the establishment of the autonomy of various regions of Being; but Husserl's subjectivism, even in Part II of the *Logical Investigations*, inevitably fostered an unacceptable idealism. It may even be the case that Husserl sees Heidegger as falling into this realistic orientation as well, for one of his marginal notes also exclaims, "Heidegger's realism."

natural attitude

Thus it is clear that from Husserl's perspective, Heidegger's phenomenology remains rooted in the naïvete of the natural attitude. As we have seen, this natural attitude presupposes the existence of the world, explicitly or implicitly. If Heidegger's thought is viewed as an anthropologism, this means that the self (*Dasein*) is still conceived as a part of the original whole, the world. But what further complicates the issue is Heidegger's own claims in *Being and Time* that the existential analytic of *Dasein* must be sharply differentiated from all psychology and anthropology. All such sciences, whether carried out on a categorial or existentiell basis, are ontic disciplines, which leave their ontological foundations in obscurity. Such disciplines must be "founded upon the ontology of Dasein";[47] that is, upon the existential analytic.

In other words, for Heidegger, philosophy is the science of Being, and a philosophical study of man's Being (*Dasein*) is the task of existential, rather than existentiell, analyses. The distinction between the ontic and the ontological, therefore, is the basis for the difference between the nonphilosophical and the philosophical. In Husserl's thought, this distinction is between the natural and the transcendental attitudes. From such a perspective, it appears that both the ontic and the ontological dimensions in Heidegger fall within the natural attitude, and hence ontological analyses must still submit to the reduction.

It is naturally naïve to say that man is a being who is conscious of all other beings as his horizon of Being, or that he has a

previous understanding of the Being of all entities, of himself
and of all other beings. . . .[48]

Again, in opposition to this, Heidegger claims that only an ontological analytic of that entity in which transcendental constitution
occurs can secure an adequate basis for an understanding of the
phenomenon of intentionality. In a letter to Husserl concerning their
collaboration on the *Encyclopaedia Britannica* article, dated October
22, 1927, Heidegger says:

> We agree that beings, in the sense of which you call the "world,"
> cannot be clarified through a return to beings of the same nature.
> But this does not mean that what determines the location of the
> transcendental is not a being at all. Rather, it leads directly to
> the problem: What is the kind of Being of the being in which
> "world" is constituted? That is the central problem of *Being and
> Time*; that is, a fundamental ontology of Dasein. It tries to show
> that the kind of Being belonging to human Dasein is totally
> different from that of all other beings . . . and consequently
> contains in itself the possibility of transcendental constitution.[49]

In other words, even the pure reflection of subjectivity on itself,
carried out within the framework of the phenomenological-transcen-
dental reduction, still discovers a being or entity which *is* intentionally.
The sense of this being, however, cannot be that of an entity which
is "in the world" in either a biological, psychological, or anthropological sense. This is also the vital point underlying Husserl's
transcendental conception of consciousness. If we call this being or
entity "consciousness," and claim that it "is," what is the meaning
of its Being?

Husserl recognizes that with respect to the content of the analyses
of transcendental subjectivity, it should parallel that of pure psychology. The concerns of pure psychology, made accessible by the
phenomenological reduction in conjunction with the eidetic reduction
are "the invariant essential structures of the total sphere of pure
mental processes."[50] The horizon within which the entity which lives
in these processes is made accessible is still the world-horizon, as
the whole to which it belongs. The transcendental reduction, as we
have seen, inverts the whole-part relationship, as the world reemerges
in all its fullness as the noematic correlate of transcendental experience.

What should be noted here, however, is that if there is this material parallelism between phenomenological psychology and transcendental phenomenological philosophy, and the subject matter of the former is a being which is worldly in the mundane sense, then the location (*Ort*) of the transcendental must still be an entity, though not in any ordinary or worldly sense of the term. One of the clear differentiations, for example, between the Kantian transcendental ego and the Husserlian transcendental subjectivity is this "ontic" identity between the mundane and transcendental ego. Thus, both psychology and philosophy will claim that "consciousness is intentional." What differentiates the psychological from the philosophical proposition? It surely cannot be the intentionality of consciousness, for both uphold it. What distinguishes them can be nothing other than the meaning of "is," the meaning of "to be," the meaning of the Being of the entity which is intentionally directed. In Cartesian terms, it is the meaning of the *sum* rather than the *cogito*.

Thus, Heidegger says:

> Transcendental constitution is a central possibility for the existence of the factical self. Concrete man as such never is as a "real, worldly fact," because man never is present-at-hand, but rather exists.[51]

The *sum* of Cartesian ontology is replaced in Heidegger with the concept of *Existenz*, which is progressively interpreted in *Being and Time* in terms of Being-in-the-World, Care, and the temporalizing of temporality. To say that *Dasein* is not a worldly thing is to claim that it never merely exists as a thing among things in the world. *Zuhandenheit* (readiness-to-hand) and *Vorhandenheit* (presence-at-hand) are two modes of Being of worldly entities, although they may not be the only two possible ones. *Dasein* never "is" in this sense, and realizes this if its self-understanding is authentic. If *Dasein* comes to comprehend itself in a "substantial" fashion, it does not thereby cease to *Exist*, but rather its movement of *Existenz* is of such a fashion as to cover over its genuine ontological nature, its ownmost potentiality-for-Being; that is, it *Exists* inauthentically.

POSING THE QUESTION OF BEING

Through these considerations we can perhaps begin to focus in on the crucial issue in the attempt to see the relationship between the transcendental phenomenology of Husserl, and the hermeneutic phenomenology of Heidegger. All of our preceding interpretation of Husserl has been directed at explicating the nature and significance of the transcendental turn in his thinking. This transcendental turn is the movement from the nonphilosophical (the worldly, naïve, mundane, or dogmatic) to the philosophical dimension. The two vital components of this movement were shown to be the concept of intuitive rationality, articulated as the principle of all principles, and as a corollary to that, the theory of wholes and parts. For when Husserl presents the highest principle, he does so in terms of givenness and its limits, that is, in terms of parts and wholes. The movement from the nonphilosophical to the philosophical in Heidegger, on the other hand, is that from the ontic to the ontological, from beings to Being. In *Being and Time*, he claims that it is phenomenology that allows us to make this move. "Phenomenology is our way of access to what is to be the theme of ontology, and it is our way of giving it demonstrative precision. Only as phenomenology, is ontology possible."[52] The vital question that needs to be taken up bears on the primordiality of these moves. In other words, it seems that from Husserl's perspective, Heidegger's fundamental ontology is still worldly or naïve, while for Heidegger, Husserl's transcendental analyses remain immersed in the ontic.

The way in which *Being and Time* begins is well known. Its starting point is the question of Being, or more precisely, the question of the meaning of Being: "What is asked about is Being—that which determines entities as entities. . . ."[53] That which does the "determining," the nature of the determining, and that which is determined, remain ambiguous. In posing this question, Heidegger wishes to seize upon its indeterminancy and ambiguity, seeing in this a positive phenomenal characteristic. Heidegger does not attempt to strike out against this indeterminancy, but rather to work with it, to allow it to unfold, to interpret it in the sense of laying-out (*Auslegung*) that which is contained within it.

What is so enigmatic about this question of Being is "not only that it lacks an answer, but that the question itself is obscure and without direction."[54] We do not even know which way to look, where to begin, or what to pursue. What Heidegger attempts is to turn back upon the question itself as a question, in a reflexive manner, and to examine the conditions for the possibility of raising this question. In this reflexive turn, the questioning of the question, the Self is first brought into vision. It is this act of reflection that bestows

ontic = being
ontological – Being

ein befragtes
ein Befragtes
ein Erfragtes

upon *Being and Time*, from the outset, its specific orientation as an existential analytic of *Dasein*. The initial task, the "fundamental" task, is to work out the question as a question, and the Self appears as the one who asks the question, as the questioner of Being, the one who *quests* after Being.

Prior to initiating the specific analysis of the *Seinsfrage*, however, Heidegger first examines the formal structures of questioning in general. A question or inquiry has a triadic formal structure: (1) that which is asked about (*ein Gefragtes*), (2) that which is interrogated (*ein Befragtes*), and (3) that which is to be found out by the asking (*ein Erfragtes*). So, for example, I can *ask about* the author of *Candide*, and *interrogate* my copy of the book, or a friend, or another book, and *find out* that it is Voltaire. As formal moments of the structure of a question, these belong to any question, whether it be of the author of *Candide* or of the meaning of Being. With regard to the basic question of ontology, that which is asked about is Being; that which is interrogated are entities or beings; and that which is to be found out by the asking is the meaning of Being.

Heidegger's next step is to move from the question, itself considered as an object or entity, to the behavior of a questioner. Questions "are" only insofar as they are asked, and hence are essentially linked up with the act of asking by the one who questions. If we put this in terms of intentional analyses, we can say that Heidegger here shifts from the noematic to the noetic side, from the question to its essential ground in the act of questioning. In disclosing the conditions for the possibility of a question, Heidegger not only uncovers a certain "objective" a priori, but a "subjective" one as well.

The final, and perhaps most important, formal characteristics of questioning is that it "must be guided beforehand by what is sought."[55] In order to ask a question meaningfully, to *be* questioning, I must have some notion of that about which I am asking, regardless of how general or indeterminate that notion may be. In asking about the author of *Candide*, I hopefully already know that "red," "plutonium," and "chemistry" are unacceptable answers. If I had no set of unacceptable answers, I could not inquire. The "soul" would be a *tabula rasa*. I would be ignorant in the Platonic sense of not knowing that I don't know. In the case of the *Seinsfrage*, what is to be found out, or what is sought, is the meaning of Being. And while I do not know what it is, my questioning must be guided by a "vague average understanding of Being."[56] This understanding of Being is a condition which makes possible questioning Being, and is elicited from the fact of questioning, which now becomes the locus for the working out of the question of Being.

The first step has now been taken in overcoming the initial indeterminacy, the topic of Paragraph 1 of *Being and Time*, by working within and laying-out that indeterminancy. Furthermore, Heidegger's "turn to the subject" has already been undertaken, not through a systematic doubt uncovering an indubitable *cogito*, but my making clear what is already entailed (as an initial set of presuppositions) in raising the question of the meaning of Being.[57]

The circular nature of the entire undertaking is immediately evident. This circle, subsequently developed as the hermeneutic circle, is present from the outset, and is disclosed as the condition for the possibility of the question of the meaning of Being, and hence for *Being and Time*. To eliminate the circle, to get out of it, is to destroy the possibility of questioning, of inquiring, of philosophizing. Thus Heidegger later says, "What is decisive is not to get out of the circle but to come into it in the right way."[58] Presumably, at this stage of his thought, Heidegger feels that *Being and Time* does "come into it in the right way." If *Being and Time* is an interpretation which in any sense succeeds, it does so "by not failing to recognize beforehand the essential conditions under which it can be performed."[59] And these conditions are both the conditions for any questioning and the conditions for questioning Being. They are:

1. "There is" Being (*Gefragtes*)
2. "There is" the meaning of Being (*Erfragtes*)
3. "There is" an entity (*Befragtes*)
4. "There is" a questioner
5. "There is" a vague, average understanding of Being

To disclose the way in which these conditions can cohere so as to make possible posing the *Seinsfrage* in a meaningful way is the task of *Being and Time*, the goal of fundamental ontology. The locus of these conditions is the "there" of Being, *Dasein*. It is in this way that we should understand the first mention of *Dasein* in *Being and Time*.

This entity which each of us is himself and which includes inquiring as one of the possibilities of its Being, we shall denote by the term "*Dasein*." If we are to formulate our question explicitly and transparently, we must first give a proper explication of an entity (*Dasein*), with regard to its Being.[60]

If any genuine ontological knowledge is to be possible, and not just that preontological understanding of Being which Heidegger says belongs to *Dasein*, it must come as an answer to the fully articulated question of the meaning of Being. Hence those conditions which make possible the question also make possible such knowledge. In *Kant and the Problem of Metaphysics*, Heidegger attempts an interpretation or retrieve of Kant's *Critique of Pure Reason* in terms of the question of the possibility of ontological knowledge, seen as the laying of the foundation for metaphysics. In doing this, he explicates the Transcendental Deduction and Schematism sections in terms of the problem of the pure synthesis of pure intuition (time) and pure thought (the notions, or *logical* categories). In describing this project, Heidegger says that "the problem of the intrinsic possibility of ontological knowledge is nothing other than the revelation of transcendence."[61] And in *The Essence of Reasons*, he asserts:

> We might point out here that the portion of the investigations concerning "Being and Time" published so far has as its task nothing more than a concrete, revealing sketch (*Entwurf*) of transcendence (cf. ##12–83, esp. #69). The sketch is there in order to make the *single* prominent goal of these investigations possible, a goal that is clearly indicated in the heading of the whole first part: viz., attaining the *transcendental* horizon of the *question* about Being.[62]

Thus, "transcendence" is the theme of *Being and Time*, the theme of *Kant and the Problem of Metaphysics*, and insofar as "the question about the essence of reasons becomes the problem of transcendence,"[63] it is the theme of *The Essence of Reasons*. In other words, the way in which the disclosure of the conditions for the possibility of the question of Being is pursued by Heidegger is in terms of the idea of transcendence.

TRANSCENDENCE AND WORLD

What, then, is transcendence? How does it make possible the question of Being, on the one hand, and ontological knowledge, on the other? And how can it serve to illuminate the relation between Husserl's transcendental phenomenology and Heidegger's hermeneutic phenomenology as a phenomenology of transcendence?

In *The Essence of Reasons*, Heidegger says that "transcendence constitutes selfhood," that "transcendence can be said to denote the essence of the subject or the basic structure of subjectivity." Hence "to be a subject means to be in and as a transcending being." This is to be understood in contrast to a subject which "first exists as 'subject,' and then, in the event objects are present at hand, goes on to transcend as well."[64] This way of introducing the notion of transcendence seems to bear a strong resemblance to Husserl's concept of intentionality. As was shown, intentionality is not a relation between two things or substances, but the movement of consciousness just insofar as it "is" at all. This similarity between the intentionality of consciousness for Husserl and transcendence of the "subject" for Heidegger, however, is only a superficial one. That toward which intentionality "tends" is always an object, in a formally broad sense. It might be a mathematical or imaginary object, or even a relation between such objects. But it is always a being, property of a being, or a horizon of possible beings. In contrast to this, Heideggerian transcendence has for its "toward-which" the World.

Once again, however, this does not seem to be so radically different from Husserl's intentionality. After all, what is the world other than the totality of beings; of cultural entities, mathematical entities, physical entities, psychological entities, and so forth? But in transcending to the World, what is transcended "are simply beings themselves (*das Seiende selbst*); that is, every being which can be or become unconcealed to *Dasein*, even and precisely the very being which, as 'it itself' exists."[65] If the world is understood as the totality of beings, then it is the world that is transcended. Thus, if we are to understand how it is possible to "define transcendence as Being-in-the-World,"[66] the different senses of "world" must be clarified.

In drawing the concept of the world into the center of our anlysis in this fashion, we reencounter the often cited antithesis between Husserl and Heidegger as to the "location" of the primordial subject: a worldless transcendental subjectivity versus Being-in-the-World. To note this as an important difference is undoubtedly correct. But simply to leave the matter at that, failing to unravel the multiple meanings of "world" in Husserl and Heidegger, is to miss the authentic sense of the contrast. We must not remain content in our analysis merely with juxtaposing words and concepts, but rather need to penetrate to the phenomena to which they refer.

We noted in passing in Chapter 3 that while Husserl is not always clear on this matter, he seems to use "world" in at least two essentially different senses. On the¹ one hand, he appears to mean the totality of objects, the sum of which, taken from all the various sections and regions, would be the world. "The world is the totality of objects that can be known through experience (*Erfahrung*), known in terms of orderly theoretical thought on the basis of direct present experience."⁶⁷ To think it in these terms is to see it as an "all," a sum or multiplicity of pieces, which may in *fact* form a unity, but which in *essence* are independent. A more developed concept of the world in Husserl, however, is that of a whole of which the different objects in the world are moments.⁶⁸ So understood, as Sokolowski notes, "the world is not a large thing. . . ."⁶⁹ Instead, it is the basis or foundation for our natural belief in the thinghood of things, in their "presence" (*Vorhandenheit*), "out there" (*da*), in their independent existence.

If we accept, in all its ambiguity, the notion of Being as that which determines entities as entities, then the natural belief in the world is a belief in Being. The world so understood is not a being or thing, but that which "is pregiven . . . in every case, in such a way that individual things are given."⁷⁰ It is this sense of the world that the transcendental reduction attempts to put out of play, and hence is a bracketing of Being. We do not individually bracket the existence of an infinite number of possible beings, but the one universal horizon which nourishes that belief in existence (Being), the world as the absolute *concretum* or final whole.

We should, therefore, recognize a very strong similarity between this second sense of the world in Husserl (world[2]), and the World as the "toward-which" of transcendence in Heidegger.⁷¹ Our belief in the world, in the natural attitude, transcends or surpasses all particular entities and the totality of entities, bestowing on those entities their Being (understood by Husserl as *Vorhandenheit*) as worldly beings. Heidegger too insists that in our transcendence to the World, we transcend the totality of beings. Heidegger, however, does not talk about our belief in the world, but rather our Being-in-the-World.

At this point we need to ask if "belief in" is an appropriate description of our relatedness to the world. I might know what it means to believe in the existence of an object, or even in the existence of the world as the totality of objects (world[1]). "The world, on the other hand, does not exist as an object, as an entity,"⁷² claims Husserl. But can it, then, be the object of any *act*, or even of an ideal totality of acts? If it *is* as world-horizon, what does it mean to *believe in* it?

I do not believe so much that it exists, but that objects within it exist, and that they owe their existence or Being to that world. It would seem, then, that what I naturally believe in is its functional significance in that I let the world operate. When I abstain from this belief, then I neutralize that functioning, although allegedly it still continues.

But does it really make sense to say that the world, in this second sense (world[2]), is rediscovered within transcendental subjectivity? Is it not the case that the meaning of the world[2] is its functioning as the source of the Being-sense of the things in the world? This neutralization of the bestowal of Being is really an "annihilation of the world." The totality of objects may still remain, as well as the infinite, internal and external horizons. But transcendental subjectivity *replaces* the world[2] as the whole on which all else depends, so that the world as a whole ceases to be. The world which is found to be constituted in transcendental subjectivity is "an idea correlative to a perfect experimental evidence, . . . a multiform horizon of unfulfilled anticipations."[73] But as such it is a totality of possible objects (world[1]), objects which receive their objectivity and Being in and through the synthetic coherence of multiple modes of appearing, that is, via transcendental subjectivity.

If we now turn to Heidegger's concept of the World, we shall finally be able to see the precise ground of difference between the worldless transcendental subjectivity of Husserl and *Dasein* as Being-in-the-World. In *Being and Time*, there is an enumeration of four different senses of the word "world," along with a specification of its meaning within the description of *Dasein's* transcendence understood as Being-in-the-World. "World" can mean (1) the totality of entities, (2) the Being of those entities, (3) the "wherein" of factual *Dasein*, and (4) the ontologico-existential concept of worldhood. The expression Being-in-the-World uses the concept in the third sense. World is thus an existentiell or anthropological concept, and can embrace such different possibilities as the ethical world, the religious world, the political world, the academic world, the domestic world, and so forth.

In *The Essence of Reasons*, Heidegger traces the way in which "world" has been understood by various authors. In looking at texts from Parmenides, Heracleitus, the New Testament, Augustine, Aquinas, the "School metaphysics" of Baumgarten and Crucius, and finally Kant, he attempts to show the many ways in which "world" has been used, both as an ontic and ontological term, as well as in a cosmological and anthropological (existentiell) sense. So, for example, in the Gospel of John, "world" means not only the totality of created things, but the "how" of man's comportment toward those things. These historical references supply a background for the four senses of "world" in *Being and Time*, where they are simply presented without such historical justifications.

It might seem that in raising the problem of the World, Heidegger is interested in articulating the various worlds in which *Dasein* can live. His concern, however, is not with these multiple world-views, but with that which makes any world a world.[74] He says that what is sought is:

> neither the common world nor the subjective world, but the worldhood of the world as such. . . . Worldhood itself may have as its modes whatever structural wholes any special "worlds" may have at the time; but it embraces in itself the a priori character of worldhood in general.[75]

The procedure, then, is to begin with a world, or rather with entities within a world, and to move toward the worldhood of the world. *Dasein* is not ontologically capatured as Being-in-a-World, but as Being-in-the-World.

The entities with which Heidegger begins, he insists, must not be interpreted as "things" *(res)*, but rather as *pragmata* or equipment *(das Zeug)*. What is it about these beings which first lets them be encountered as they are "in themselves"? Heidegger recognizes that prior to our encounter with equipment or tools is the Being of that equipment, and our encounter and contact with, or understanding of, that Being. His claim, however, is that traditional ontology tries to explain this by transforming the *pragmata* into "things," into other types of beings, into substances. Prior to our grasping them as things for use, they must be just things. This move, however, attempts to explain the foundation for the ontic within the ontic. If one fails to grasp what Heidegger calls the ontological difference, then this mode of explanation seems necessary. Any use to which we put things must be founded upon their Being as things.

While Heidegger shares with traditional ontology the recognition of the inadequacy of the ontic status of *Zeuge* (equipment), he does not try to supplement or found it on some other ontic status (substances); but rather on the Being of *Zeuge*, which itself is not any being. The Being of equipment is readiness-to-hand, and its structure "is determined by references or assignments *(Verweisungen)*."[76] Equipment is essentially something "in order to" *(um-zu)*. Whether this be a hammer, a chair, a sheet of paper, a typewriter, etc., they are all *for* something; they possess an "in-order-to." Lying within this *um-zu* are manifold references, such as the toward-which of the work, the where-of of the materials, and ultimately that for-the-sake-of-which the work is, *Dasein* itself. In describing these manifold references or assignments, and hence the Being of the ready-to-hand, Heidegger uses the term "involvement." I can be *involved with* papers, pencils, ink, a desk, a chair, a lamp, and so on, *in* the work of writing an essay, *for the sake of* someone else's, or my own, understanding. I can be *involved* with wrenches, screwdrivers, pliers, spark plugs, etc., *in* the task of repairing my car, *for the sake of* my transportation. In each case, what makes possible the encounter with the various beings is a prior familiarity with, disclosure or understanding of, this totality of involvements.

Heidegger introduces the understanding *(Verstehen)* as that which discloses these references, which "holds itself in them with familiarity, and in so doing, it holds them *before* itself." The way in which these references are bound together is one of "signifying," and "the relational totality of this signifying we call significance." Heidegger thus comprehends the World as follows:

> The "wherein" of an understanding which assigns or refers itself is that for which one lets entities be encountered in the kind of Being that belongs to involvements; and this "wherein" is the phenomenon of the world. And the structure of that to which Dasein assigns itself is what makes up the worldhood of the world.[77]

This structure is significance, and *Dasein's* familiarity with it "goes to make up *Dasein's* understanding of Being."[78] These involvements, understood ontologically as references, are not one-sidedly founded on the beings which are involved, but *found* them ontologically as the beings they are.[79]

Thus transcendence, as Being-in-the-World, is nothing other than the prior disclosedness of the structurally articulated totality of significance which makes possible all encounters with beings. It transcends the totality of beings in first allowing them "to be": to be *involved*, to be *present*, to *Exist*. This disclosedness is the "there" of Being, *Da*-sein. It is the understanding of Being which belongs to the questioner of Being as the condition for the possibility of questioning the meaning of Being. We still work within the circle, simply developing and radicalizing our preontological understanding of Being: for "philosophical thought takes place as the explicit transcendence of Dasein."[80]

The most important point to be recognized here is that any encounter with a being or entity, whether it be a practical, theoretical, ethical, aesthetic, or political one, always works within a prior understanding of the Being of the entity encountered, and is made possible by that understanding. And this understanding (*Verstehen*) is implied in transcendence or Being-in-the-World. So with regard to equipment and readiness-to-hand, Heidegger says, "Being-in-the-World . . . amounts to a nonthematic circumspective absorption in references *constitutive* for the *Zuhandenheit* of a totality of equipment."[81] More radically, however,

> all the modes of Being of entities within-the-world are founded ontologically upon the worldhood of the world, and accordingly upon the phenomenon of Being-in-the-World. From this there arises the insight that among the modes of Being of entities within-the-World, Reality has no priority, and that Reality is a kind of Being which cannot even characterize anything like the world or Dasein in a way which is ontologically appropriate.[82]

Here we a find Heideggerian analogue to the inversion of the meaning of Being, but with the "ontological foundation" now being *Dasein*, rather than transcendental subjectivity.

Husserl wishes to trace the problem of Being back to the intentional (constitutive) achievements of transcendental subjectivity. These analyses will disclose the Being of the world [1] as totality of possible objects, *and* the Being of the transcendental ego in its self-constitution. The flow of consciousness, in its essential synthetic structure, not only achieves the identity of the objects meant as noematic correlate, but also the identity of the ego which lives in and through these acts. The structure of transcendental subjectivity is not just *cogito-cogitatum*, but *ego-cogito-cogitatum*. This subjective, self-constitution results not only in an empty, self-identical ego pole, but also in a "substrate of habitualities," giving the ego an essential style or "personal character."[83] Thus the full (whole), monadically concrete transcendental ego embraces both directions of the intentional syntheses, constituting itself in these syntheses according to essential laws, such that

> the activity of positing and explicating Being sets up a habituality of my ego by virtue of which the object, as having its manifold determinations, is mine abidingly.[84]

Thus Husserl can conclude:

> the problem of explicating this monadic ego phenomenologically (the problem of his constitution for himself) must include all constitutional problems without exception. Consequently, the phenomenology of this self-constitution coincides with phenomenology as a whole.[85]

But from Heidegger's position, constitutive analyses, whether objectively or subjectivity directed, do not achieve an insight into the Being of beings. Rather, they presuppose it. So with regard to objective constitution, Heidegger says:

> If one characterizes every comportment toward beings as intentional, then intentionality is possible only on the basis of transcendence. It is neither identical with transcendence nor that which makes transcendence possible.[86]

Transcendence is Being-in-the-World, and the latter does *not* denote an intentional relationship. Nor does an alteration of attitudes toward the being which "is" intentionally give us transcendence.

We find Heidegger emphasizing the same point in his lectures from the Summer semester of 1927, recently published under the title *Die Grundprobleme der Phänomenologie*. In the first part of these lectures, he uses the concept of intentionality to disclose a basic, and perhaps essential ambiguity in the notion of perception found in Kant's philosophy. At the same time, he shows the inadequacy of intentionality, as a directedness to beings, to the problem of the Being of those beings. Intentionality can function only as the first step toward the onotological dimension, in the movement from the ontic to the ontological. But the structure of intentionality itself is ontologically grounded in the basic structure of *Dasein* (Being-in-the-World).[87] Heidegger says,

> To the intentionality of perception belongs not only the *intentio* and the *intentum*, but also the understanding of the Being of that which is intended in the *intentum*.[88]

Buried within or beneath intentionality, which gives us beings, is the Being of intentionality, the Being of the subject, the understanding of Being: the disclosedness of Being *founds*, that is, provides the ground or foundation for the possibility of the discoveredness of beings.[89]

This same criticism of objective constitution would be directed at subjective, self-constitution as well. For example, in talking about Husserl and Scheler, Heidegger notes their agreement that the "person" is not a thing or substance, "that the unity of the person must have a *constitution* different from that required for the unity of things of nature."[90] But Heidegger goes on to mention the failure of such analyses to enter the ontological dimension.

> The phenomenological interpretation of personality is in principle more radical and more transparent (vs. Dilthey and Bergson); but the question of the Being of Dasein has a dimension which this too fails to enter. . . . Acts get performed; the person is a performer of acts. What, however, is the ontological meaning of "performance"? How is the kind of Being which belongs to the performer to be ascertained in a positive way?[91]

While the unity of the person and of the object are different, they still both arise as the unity *constituted* through syntheses in the temporal flow of consciousness.

From Heidegger's perspective, any type of constitutive analysis, whether it focus on the relation between *cogitationes* and *cogitata* or between *cogitationes* and *ego*, still thematizes a being, an act, and thus already presupposes the Being of the act, and understands its Being in a certain fashion. And insofar as the unity constituted through the synthesis of acts is a moment "within" the structure *ego-cogito-cogitatum*, the Being of that unity, whether it be object or person, is already understood. Husserl wishes to replace the concept of the world [2] with transcendental subjectivity, insofar as the latter constitutes the world [1] and thus supplies beings with their Being. The multiple modes of appearing in transcendental subjectivity replace the world [2], as that which determines entities as entities. If there is a kind of ontological difference between Being and beings in Husserl, then transcendental subjectivity is Being.

But, from Heidegger's perspective, any real ontological difference collapses insofar as the transcendental subject is still a being. When the acts of this subject are grasped in reflection, they are entities, though perhaps no longer the acts of a worldly entity. Heidegger would agree with Husserl on this point, that the primordial subject is not just another being alongside other beings within-the-world. Any anthropological approach is philosophically inadequate. But the self or subject still is Being-in-the-World, transcending to the World as the possibility for encountering objects, as well as the subject of reflection. Being-in-the-World is also the condition for the possibility of the act of reflection which grasps another act as belonging to the same stream. This reflective act must anticipate or project the Being of the reflected act; it must understand its own Being. An understanding of its own Being belongs essentially to *Dasein*. The acts grasped transcendentally may no longer be grasped as those of human (worldly) consciousness or psychic life, but to be grasped *as* acts, their "acthood" must be already understood. Any consistent idealism must recognize that "the ontological analysis of consciousness itself is prescribed as an inevitable *prior* task."[92]

The neutralization of the belief in the world[2] effected by the transcendental reduction attempts to make us cognizant of our prior understanding of the Being of entities, which Husserl describes in terms of "naïve belief." We must transcend this prior understanding so that we can witness its birth in transcendental subjectivity and in the achievements of the acts of that subject. But to suspend *belief in* the Being of entities understood in a certain fashion is not to escape and stand outside the understanding of Being, but simply to modify our Being-in-the-World. The neutralization of "belief in" is not an overcoming of the "understanding of" or the "Being-in."[93] Being as believed in is only one way of concretizing the understanding of Being (*Seinsverständnis*). The task of making consciousness explictly *present* to itself, whether as a part of the whole or as the whole, still understands Being as Being-present. That Being-present is now no longer pregiven, but is seen as the result of syntheses of identity, and as a task or goal set for consciousness. But each moment of that synthesis, and the whole constituted in it, is already understood as Being-present, the *tending* toward full presence by that which is partially present.

The interweaving of the modes of presence and absence which unfold in the flow of conscious life testifies to this prior understanding of Being. Even the ideal of pure intuition is held by Heidegger to be the noetic correlate of the ontological priority of pure presence-at-hand. We have seen that presence and abence are descriptive of the way in which the whole-part relationship functions; one sees what is given (present) within the limits of its givenness (absent as emptily intended). Thus the two most basic factors underlying the transcendental turn in Husserl, the principle of all principles and the theory of wholes and parts, are based upon a prior understanding of Being. Being means being present as an object of an act, whether that act be transcendently or immanently directed. This is what was meant earlier in saying that the transcendental reduction fails to illuminate its own presuppositions.

Just how thoroughly Husserl's philosophy works within this understanding of Being can be seen if we remember the way in which the initial question of his philosophy is posed. In Chapter 2 we saw this question articulated precisely in terms of *evidence*. If the question of Being is posed in terms of the discovery of those evidences which are first in themselves, as *founding*, then it is not surprising that the analyses of the constitutive achievements of intentionality claim to solve the question of Being. For in *Formal and Transcendental Logic*, Husserl explicitly says that evidence "is *the universal* preeminent form of intentionality."[94] Thus all consciousness is thereby evidential as well. In asking the *first* question in this fashion, Husserl assumes that the way in which Being determines entities as entities is in terms of evidential foundation, a making present of identity through multiplicity. In making the foundational beginnings *evidential*, Husserl takes ontological foundations in terms of syntheses of identity. The inversion of the meaning of Being, while making Reality subordinate ontologically, still functions within the understanding of Being as pure presence-at-hand. For evidence is "the act of [the] most perfect synthesis of fulfillment . . .; the object is not merely meant but in the strictest sense *given* and given as it is meant."[95]

These criticisms, however, should not be taken as diminishing the significance of the concept of intentionality, nor as a dismissal of intentional analysis. The discovery of the intentionality of consciousness gives us an initial access to the phenomenon of Being-in-the-World. All ontological analyses begin with the ontic, the Being of an *entity*, and work out the understanding of the Being of that entity which becomes accessible on the basis of that understanding. The phenomenological reduction, in giving us the intentionality of the phenomena, discloses the inappropriate nature of a substance ontology for the comprehension of subjectivity.

With the discovery of intentionality in "this sense" the simultaneous thematization of "beings in the how of their being given, for the first time in the history of philosophy" is found "expressly and clearly the basis for a radical ontological investigation."[96]

The very concept of "subject" itself is shaken by the notion of intentionality.

In Paragraph 64 of *Being and Time* one finds a "history of modern philosophy" from a Heideggerian perspective, reminiscent of Aristotle's reflections on the treatment of the "causes" (*aition*) by his predecessors. Four distinct conceptions of subjectivity are presented in this section of *Being and Time*, corresponding to the positions of Descartes, Kant, Husserl, and finally Heidegger himself.[97] With the introduction of the Kantian notion of the pure "I think" which necessarily accompanies all presentations as the transcendental unity of apperception, a certain "dynamizing" of the Self occurs. In the Paralogisms, Kant overcomes the idea of the self as substance characteristic of Cartesian rationalism. The "I" is not something which can or does think, and underlies these activities as substratum (*hypokeimenon*). The "I" *is* "I think" as a "binding together."

Heidegger's claim, however, is that a substance ontology still constrains and cuts short the Kantian advancement, insofar as Kant conceived of this "I think" as something which accompanies all presentations. The accompanying of the Self with the presentations is left ontologically indeterminate. "At bottom, however, their kind of Being is understood as the constant Being-present-at-hand of the 'I' along with its presentation."[98] It is at this juncture that Heidegger introduces the Husserlian notion of intentionality as an internally articulated triadic unity. With this concept, the self is not only kept in essential unity with activity, but this activity itself becomes "meaningful." In other words, the Self becomes an activity which lives meaningfully toward the meant. This is the essence of the Husserlian doctrine of intentionality, that the eidetic structure of transcendental subjectivity is *ego-cogito-cogitatum*. The movement from substance to subject becomes complete.

With this type of abbreviated historical account as a backdrop, Heidegger introduces his own position, or the ground for it, precisely in terms of the notion of World. The "something thought" is necessarily something within-the-World; and it is this World that functions as the a priori condition for the possibility of intentionality as such. Heidegger's relation to Husserl, therefore, discloses itself here in terms of a ground of continuity. *Being and Time* seeks the ontological presuppositions for a doctrine of intentionality, and does so in terms of Being-in-the-World and its meaning.

Thus, from the Heideggerian perspective, the transcendental reduction must be seen as superfluous. If its intention is to uncover the ultimate field of origins, Being in the sense of that which determines entities as entities, it must fail. Constitutive analyses still deal with entities, remaining at the ontic level, and working within an unclarified understanding of Being. Thus Husserl's phenomenology has a prior commitment to "a particular way of raising and answering fundamental metaphysical questions concerning Being, the meaning of Being, and the different modes of Being."[99]

5

Phenomenological Beginnings

A SUMMARY

W HAT HAS BEEN ATTEMPTED in this work is a redirection of
thinking concerning the relationship between the phenomenologies of Husserl and Heidegger. For serious reflection
on this matter to arise, it must take its ground in the nature of the
problematics which these thinkers confront. If genuine, philosophical
ties exist between Husserl and Heidegger, then these must be uncovered in the underlying subject matter which their thinking ad-
dresses. The establishment of historical connections in the way of
teacher-pupil relations, observations concerning similarities and differences in language, the discovery of personal conflicts and tensions
rooted in the social and political climate of the age, while being
legitimate themes for scholarly research, are extraneous to the essence
of philosophical interpretation. The fact, for example, that Husserl
was a mathematician may help us to understand certain aspects of
his thinking if our questions concern the factual, historical, or psychological genesis of his thought. But the securing of such facts in
no way establishes the meaning or merit, the truth or falsehood, of
Husserl's philosophy. We must always attend to the essentials of the
matters thought, of "the things themselves," rather than the inci-
dentals accompanying them.

That the advent of the transcendental reduction marks *the* decisive
stage in the development of Husserl's phenomenology is largely
undisputed. As a consequence of this reduction, descriptive psychology (*Logical Investigations*) becomes constitutive phenomenology
(*Ideas I*), and ultimately transcendental idealism (*Cartesian Meditations*). We have tried to show a way in which the transcendental
reduction can be comprehended by disclosing the nature of the

problem to which it is a response. In other words, what is the question to which the transcendental reduction provides an answer?

Motives for the transcendental reduction were sought, not in the antecedent historical circumstances of Husserl's formal training, nor in his growing familiarity with neo-Kantianism, but rather in the philosophical *telos* animating his project as a whole. What we have aimed at, in the words of Gaston Berger, is "a study which does not originate from outside, by considering a thought as a succession of events, but which insists on finding it (the meaning of the thought) from within."[1]

The Cartesian element in Husserl's philosophy all too readily provides an answer to this question of the guiding *telos*. But we must show restraint concerning "ready" answers. For what, according to Husserl, is living in Descartes? And what is dead? It is the ideal of science, as we have shown, that is alive. But should this ideal—first articulated in "Philosophy as Rigorous Science," implicitly functioning in *Ideas I*, and dealt with at great length in the *Cartesian Meditations*—be identified with the quest for certitude? Is it really the case that, "the concept of certitude can be regarded as the key to Husserl's thought"?[2]

We have tried to establish, via a careful textual exegesis of the preeminently "Cartesian" works of Husserl, that the matter cannot be stated so simply. The notion of the absolute of consciousness in *Ideas I*, and that of an absolute beginning point or evidence in the *Cartesian Meditations*, are not two distinct concepts, but one ideal formulated in two different manners. Is this the ideal of apodicticity? Yes and no.

The importance of the concept of certitude in Husserl's though cannot be denied. Such a project would be sheer folly. Husserl indeed hopes to establish a methodology which will allow us to found our judgments about reality, as well as our judgments about those judgments (our reflexive, philosophical judgments). Such a movement among relative evidences presupposes an ideal limit, *at least* as a regulative idea. If I claim "Experience is relative" to be a true statement, then I am rationally committed to giving an account of the position from which that judgment is made. And the content of the judgment must not exclude the possibility of that position. "Experience is relative" is a perfectly possible claim. But that "All is relative," as Aristotle knew quite well,[3] is self-contradictory. The search for such a nonrelative evidence (as apodictic) is unquestionably important in Husserl's writings.

But the basic philosophical significance of Husserl's turn to transcendental subjectivity does not lie in this dimension. The transcendental absolute must be differentiated from an epistemological absolute. Our key concept in distinguishing the two was provided by the idea of *foundation*, taken from the *Logical Investigations*, and applied analogically to the movement to transcendental subjectivity. The idea of foundation, rooted in the distinction between different types of parts and wholes, offers a concept of an absolute foundation which is an *absolute Whole*. Certain objects are essentially fragmentary or partial, and hence essentially dependent. What is it that satisfies the criteria of absolute foundation, as being that upon which all else is essentially dependent? For Husserl, it is neither things, nor the world, but transcendental subjectivity. Thus, what was attempted in Chapter 3 (under the heading, "Toward a Logic of the Transcendental Reduction") was a possible explication of what Fink suggests in his article, "Vergegenwärtigung und Bild":

Without leaving the natural attitude one could show how the *problems of totality* of the natural world, pursued to their root, end up instigating the passage to the transcendental attitude.[4]

Such an approach allows us to see the fundamental question in Husserl to be that of comprehending or understanding, not securing objectivity. In inquiring into that which constitutes an object as an object, a being as a being, Husserl is attempting to understand the Being of beings. Thus we can say that for Husserl transcendental subjectivity is Being itself, just insofar as it determines beings as beings. The ideal that this claim be apodictic remains vital for Husserl, yet it is not the meaning of the transcendental reduction itself. In fact, it tends to obscure the genuine intention of the reduction by directly assimilating it to a neo-Cartesianism. If the significance of Husserl's phenomenology were dependent upon the definitive securing of apodicticity, then it might well be the case that "the dream is over."[5] But if its significance lies more in another direction, then dialogue and criticism must orient itself from that other locus. This is the approach taken in Chapter 4, in comparing Husserl and Heidegger.

The central theme in a dialogue between these two thinkers would be that of the adequacy of transcendental, phenomenological analyses for the comprehension of the Being of beings. The problem of the "origin of the world" is a more Husserlian formulation of this question of Being. "It is," in the words of Fink, "man's eternal question concerning the origin of things which myth, religion, theology, and philosophical speculation each answer in their own way."⁶ Husserl and Heidegger agree on the deficient nature of traditional,

> basic, metaphysical notions which express the relationship of world-ground and world along the lines of intramundane relations of one being to another (for example: ground and consequent, creation and production).⁷

For Heidegger explicitly says, as has been noted: "We agree that beings, in the sense of that which you call 'world,' cannot be clarified through a return to beings of the same nature."⁸ But from Heidegger's position, transcendental analyses of the life of consciousness, whether they be of theoretical or pretheoretical life (*Lebenswelt*), focus upon intentional acts and the genesis of their objective correlates. Throughout, however, the Being of those acts, as well as the Being of the subject of those acts, is presupposed.⁹

For Heidegger, accordingly, intentional analyses of *any* sort do not achieve the genuine philosophical (ontological) domain. And no change in "attitudes" or "standpoints" will alter this state of affairs. For the ontological problematic lies in a new and *different* dimension, this difference being the ontological difference. Heidegger sees the access to this domain as being achieved hermeneutically, through an interpretation as a "laying-out" of that prior understanding of Being. If the sphere of origins escapes transcendental reflection, this suggests that the way of questioning which leads to transcendental phenomenology might itself be deficient. A philosophical treatment and critique of Husserl's phenomenology , for Heidegger, would attempt to lay out that understanding of Being which underlies the basic question of Husserlian thought.

If all questions, including philosophical questions, are possible only on the basis of a "prior knowledge," then what prior knowledge or understanding guides the development of Husserl's phenomenology? What we have shown is that the logic of wholes and parts in conjunction with the principle of all principles function as the implicit norms governing the movement to transcendental subjectivity. On the noematic side, we find a "theory of objects" yielding the concept of foundation. On the noetic side, correlated with this, is the principle of intuitive givenness within the limits of that givenness. These two factors, for Husserl, constitute the ideal of intelligibility, an ideal rooted in an understanding of Being as Being-present. This prior understanding, however, is never made explicit in Husserl, for transcendental subjectivity assumes that status of Being itself. And while this subjectivity is not considered a worldly or mundane being, it still is a being. Thus, a being usurps the role of Being, and the ontological difference is covered over.

But can transcendental subjectivity suffice as a domain of authentic origins? And does the question of Being articulated as a search for *foundations* in the Husserlian sense provide a proper beginning question? As has been continually emphasized, the problem of how philosophy begins, of what constitutes the first or initial question, and of the presuppositions of that question, are matters of central importance. Let us now try to summarize the results of our analyses by focusing upon the idea of phenomenological beginnings in Husserl and Heidegger. As has been established, the question for both is the question of Being, understood as that which determines entities as entities. Such an approach will serve to illuminate the different manner in which the *Seinsfrage* is posed by each, and the divergent conceptions of the nature of philosophical thinking which results.

A TRANSCENDENTAL OR HERMENEUTIC BEGINNING?

Perhaps the best way to pursue this issue is to look to what would constitute a Husserlian critique of Kant. This provides a fertile ground upon which to develop the problem because of the central role of the Transcendental Aesthetic in Kant's philosophy, and the antithetical interpretations of its status given by Husserl and Heidegger. It is the Transcendental Aesthetic, as Kant's beginning point, which Husserl takes to be the fatal presupposition plaguing the development of the *Critique of Pure Reason*. Heidegger, on the other hand, sees in the Aesthetic a definite establishment of the *finitude* of human knowledge, a finitude which no authentic philosophizing can afford to overlook. How then do these two thinkers come to their views on the Transcendental Aesthetic? What can be learned about the problem of beginnings from this? And what are the consequences of these views for the nature of the philosophical activity itself?

The first question of philosophy for Kant assumes the form, "How are synthetic judgments possible a priori?"[10] Two characteristics should be noted. First, the judgment is taken to be the seat of knowledge, whether it be pure or empirical. Secondly, genuine knowledge is a priori; that is, universal and necessary. If we are to know something about beings a priori, this cannot arise exclusively from sensuous experience. Thus, the question bears on the essence or possibility of a knowledge "independent" from experience. Kant, as is well known, does not try to supplement experience, which may foster only *doxa*, via a knowledge (*episteme*) directed to another realm, a realm, for example, populated by the purely intelligible Forms or Ideas. Instead, he looks to the structures of our experiencing, calling

> that knowledge transcendental which is concerned not so much with objects, as with our mode of knowledge of objects insofar as this mode of knowledge is to be possible a priori.[11]

The way in which this question of the possibility of a priori synthetic judgments becomes formulated and developed, however, is crucial, for it testifies to the preunderstanding of the "questioned" as such. This understanding, put very briefly, has to do with whether objects conform to our knowledge, or whether our knowledge must conform to objects. Expressing the problem in this manner most clearly articulates the nature of the Copernican Revolution introduced in philosophy by Kant. Kant begins the *Critique of Pure Reason* with the *hypothesis* that it might be more beneficial to develop the possibility that objects must conform to our forms of knowledge.

But from a Husserlian perspective, it could be objected that both of these alternatives, either the pre-Copernican or Copernican, are worldly or mundane formulations of the problem of knowledge. And ultimately, for Husserl, because of the anthropological nature of the concept of *human* knowledge, Kant's final position is actually a transcendental psychologism.[12] The Kantian hypothesis, that objects must conform to our knowledge, is simply the opposite pole of a relation which always presupposes the nature of knowledge, and hence to a degree, the nature of the knower and the known. Husserl would agree with the Hegelian thesis that it cannot be assumed from the outset that knowledge is an *instrument* for taking possession of the absolute, whether that instrument be creative, receptive, or a combination of the two.[13]

Rudolph Boehm suggests that Husserl sees in Kant, as the background for this manner of formulating the problem, a presupposition about the nature of beings and their "knowability."[14] Thus, Husserl might attribute to Kant an implicit argument such as the following:

1. To every being there belongs (in principle) the possibility of an adequate intuition, that is, of an intuition which would grasp the object absolutely, as it is in itself.
2. But man does not have adequate intuitions of transcendent beings.
3. Therefore, this "failure" has its source in the finitude of our intuitive capacities.

In order to *receive* beings, we must *project*, initially, space and time as mediating instruments making possible experience.

Husserl would attack Premise (1) in this argument claiming it to be no more than a naturalistic prejudice, rooted in an unclarified conception of beings and knowledge. His own phenomenological analyses of the Being of transcendent entities disclose, according to Husserl, that such a mode of "adequate givenness" would be contrary to objects' Being-sense. In *Ideas I*, he says:

> To remain forever incomplete (and hence inadequate) . . . is an ineradicable essential of the correlation Thing and Thing-perception. . . . In principle, a margin of determinable indeterminacy always remains over, however far we go along our empirical way, and however extended the continua of actual perceptions of the same thing which we may have treasured. No God can alter this in any way, any more than he can the equation $1 + 2 = 3$, or the stability of any other essential truth.[15]

As we said previously, that *things* can only be encountered through an ongoing series of perspectives is based on the meaning of the Being of things.[16] To know a "thing" all at once is not to know a "thing."

If we look to the above argument attributed to Kant, it should be noted that human finitude is a conclusion drawn from a pregiven conception of the nature of beings, in conjunction with the fact of inadequacy. But the former is really the idea of the absolute Being of the transcendent, of reality (*Wirklichkeit*), posited in the natural attitude. The vehicle for the elimination of this prejudice is the transcendental reduction, in which we refrain from all metaphysical suppositions. Husserl would view this premise as a hidden presupposition underlying Kant's philosophy. It is the presupposition which provides for the necessity of a Transcendental Aesthetic that looks to the conditions under which objects can be "given." A certain understanding of knowledge, and more radically of beings, is presupposed and supplies the foundation for the manner in which philosophical questioning develops.

A similar point is brought out very clearly in Heidegger's Kant interpretation. The receptivity of intuition is singled out as testimony to the finitude of knowledge (reason), and provides the occasion for the spontaneous, discursive activity of understanding. The "fact" of finitude necessitates conceptual determination. At the level of pure or a priori knowledge, it generates the problem of the "ontological synthesis" which, according to Heidegger, is the central issue of the *Critique of Pure Reason*. But is it not the case that the question of the conformity of the object to our knowledge, the thrust of Kant's Copernican Revolution, is simply the converse of the traditional knowledge problem?

From Husserl's perspective, once more, both formulations of the question of philosophy are inadequate in that they fail to maintain the radicalness demanded by the nature of philosophy, a radicalness allegedly achieved via the transcendental reduction. Husserl's correlation a priori is precisely the attempt to overcome the seductively apparent exhaustive disjunction which Kant poses to the Western philosophical tradition. In terms of broad, historical generalizations, Husserl's position attempts to supply a third alternative to either an objective a priori (ancient philosophy) or a subjective a priori (modern philosophy).

If the problem of knowledge, be it of pure or empirical knowledge, is posed by Kant in terms of the poles of receptivity and spontaneity, and human or finite reason is contrasted with a nondiscursive, creative intuition (*archetypus intellectus*), this is due to the ultimate source of the problematic in the "belief" that all beings are, in principle, capable of being brought to adequate intuition. If this metaphysical assumption is subjected to phenomenological criticism, as Husserl attempts, and is disclosed as fallacious, as Husserl claims, then the argument to finitude collapses. The premise upon which it is based is an artificial construction or abstraction, not rooted in the things themselves.

Our problem, however, bears not on the relationship between Husserl and Kant, but rather on that between Husserl and Heidegger. Yet the former's importance in this context lies in the fact that for Heidegger too, the concept of finitude is central. The locus of finitude in the *Critique* lies in the Transcendental Aesthetic. But if the background of the Aesthetic, and consequently of the opposition between receptivity and spontaneity, is a fallacious presupposition regarding beings as such (the natural attitude), then does this not undermine any philosophy based on a concept of human finitude? In particular, does it not threaten Heidegger's position, which explicitly points back to Kant? Would not such a philosophy be inherently anthropological, and hence only a partial or regional science? Would it not constitute a surreptitious elevation of man to the status of "measure of all things"? This, of course, is just the claim that Husserl levels not only against Kant, but against Heidegger as well.

But does Heidegger's philosophy begin with such worldly presuppositions? Is this "natural attitude" the hidden source of the concept of finitude in Heidegger too? If we recall the beginning of *Being and Time*, we recognize that the question of Being is asked by one who seeks an understanding of the meaning of Being. There are surely presuppositions which guide the question. But the task of hermeneutic phenomenology, and the manner in which Heidegger proceeds in *Being and Time*, is to uncover those presuppositions which are necessary for the posing of the question of the meaning of Being. What is it that supplies the possibility for the meaningful questioning of Being? It is the preontological understanding of Being.

Thus Heidegger does not attempt to answer the question as formulated in a definitive manner, for all such "definiteness" is achieved at the expense of a lack of serious philosophical reflection. Heidegger does not seek an evidence which is first in itself as *foundational*, nor does he ask how synthetic judgments are possible a priori. Instead, *Being and Time* attempts to disclose the horizon which makes possible the prior understanding, and hence the questioning, of the meaning of Being.

But that understanding of Being which makes possible the question is the Being of the questioner (Dasein), which all of us already implicitly understand just insofar as we "are," insofar as we *Exist*. Our meaningful *concern* about possibilities, or our cold indifference to possibilities as a negative mode of this concern, testifies to this understanding. The task of the existential analytic is to make this Being explicit, to interpret it. This understanding is possible insofar as Dasein is Being-in-the World, transcending to the World in what Heidegger terms Care (*Sorge*), whose meaning and unity is ultimately grasped as temporality.

The central feature, then, distinguishing this approach from the Husserlian is the phenomenon of *being already in* an understanding of Being. The necessary ontological presuppositions are not something to be eliminated, nor can they be suspended or put out of play; for they constitute the condition for the possibility of intelligibility or meaning at all. This is to recognize that, "only what stands under anticipations can be understood at all, and not what one simply confronts as something unintelligible."[17]

To situate the distinction between transcendental and hermeneutic phenomenology in the ontological difference is correct, but it must be remembered that the "ground of the ontological difference (is) the transcendence of Dasein."[18] The phenomenon of "being already in" guides the entire problematic, and is first evidenced in the analyses of the question as a question. It becomes developed in the course of *Being and Time* under such themes as facticity, thrownness, and historicality. It is the ultimate testimony to the finitude of the Being of Dasein. Dasein is already situated in the midst of beings and already is in an understanding of Being.

But this knowledge (perhaps better, understanding) of finitude will itself be finite, for it too works within the circle of all intelligibility, of all meaning, of all *Existence.* When Heidegger discloses the meaning of the Being of Dasein as Care, and finds its unity in the unity of temporality, he actually returns to the beginning point of *Being and Time,* the question of the meaning of Being. For questioning itself has an inherently temporal (and hence historical) nature. This is obviously not meant in the sense that questioning, considered as a psychological process, takes time. To place an event in time, and to measure it "with regard to before and after,"[19] is to understand the Being of that event as *Vorhandenheit,* as presence-at-hand. But the temporality of Care is not the same as the time of objects, for temporality makes possible our encounters with objects, which then can assume such determinations as past, present, and future.

In questioning Being, we are guided *beforehand* by a *prior* understanding, and vaguely *anticipate* the answer as a *possibility* to be realized. Hence, as indicated by our emphases, the element of the future appears. But the possibilities projected are given, limited possibilities. Such a limitation or contraction of possibilities is just as necessary for meaningful questioning as the element of projection. The two are inseparable. They are *momenta* in the full sense. Such limitations testify to the facticity of Dasein, to the past of temporality. Here is the "thrown" dimension of the thrown project. And furthermore, in questioning Being, some being is always interrogated. The presence of that which is interrogated constitutes the meaning of the temporal present, and the dimension of "fallenness." It is this primordial temporality, in the unity of the *ecstases* of time, which makes possible the concernful questioning of Being, and which is the meaning of Care. A being who is concerned, who *needs* to question, is a finite being, a being who philosophizes.[20]

Thus, in *Kant and the Problem of Metaphysics* Heidegger develops the "metaphysics of Dasein . . . as the problem of the finitude in man."[21] He says, for example,

> In transcendence, Dasein manifests itself as the need for the comprehension (understanding) of Being. This need assures (*sorgt*) the possibility of something on the order of Dasein. This need is nothing other than finitude in its most intrinsic form as that which is the source of Dasein.[22]

Heidegger even goes so far as to characterize "finitude as the understanding of Being."[23] With this theme of finitude, Heidegger sees himself reviving (retrieving) the authentic sense of Kant's Transcendental Aesthetic. He does not do this, however, by focusing on the receptivity of intuition. Notions such as receptivity and spontaneity presuppose certain types of relations between subject and object. Husserl rightly rejects these ideas as being mundane, worldly concepts. But Heidegger nonetheless insists upon the legitimacy of the Aesthetic against all attempts to "logicize" it.

Heidegger does not presuppose our ontological finitude by beginning with definitions of faculties of knowledge as does Kant in the Transcendental Aesthetic.[24] He does not presuppose these modes of relation to objects. In *Kant and the Problem of Metaphysics*, Heidegger is careful to draw the distinction between an ontic and an ontological concept of finitude. He says, for example:

> Human intuition . . . is not "sensible" (thus finite) because its affection takes place through sense organs. Rather the converse is true; it is because our Dasein is finite—existing in the midst of the essent which already is and to which our Dasein is abandoned—that it must of necessity receive the essent, that is offer it the possibility of giving notice of itself.[25]

On the basis of this, Heidegger asserts, "Kant was the first to arrive at an *ontological*, nonsensuous concept of sensibility."[26] The finitude here defined is not grounded in the fact (ontic) of the receptivity of intuition. Instead, as Heidegger says, man is receptive, and hence ontically finite and dependent because he is ontologically finite.

Thus, Heidegger wants to move away from an anthropological or psychological concept of finitude, which may indeed lead to a transcendental psychologism, to an ontological idea of finitude. His interest is in uncovering the "Dasein in man," the Being of man. "More primordial than man is the finitude of the Dasein in him."[27] This is to say that the ontic encounter with beings at the level of sensuous intuition, or of dealings with equipment as explicated in *Being and Time*, is made possible by the prior understanding of the Being of those beings.

> The comprehension of Being (*Seinsverständnis*) which dominates human existence, although man is unaware of its breadth, constancy, and indeterminateness, is . . . manifest as the innermost ground of human finitude.[28]

By beginning, therefore, with the question of Being, and showing that it *needs* to be asked, and that it can be asked only on the basis of a prior understanding of Being, he discloses our finitude "phenomenologically." Gadamer perhaps puts it best in saying the following:

> Dasein that projects itself in relation to its own potentiality-for-being has always "been." This is the meaning of the existential of "thrownness." The main point of the hermeneutics of facticity and its contrast with the transcendental constitution research of Husserl's phenomenology was that no freely chosen relation towards one's own being can go back beyond the facticity of this being.[29]

Thus, the "whole" for Heidegger, the "essence of grounds," is an essentially finite one. We find no absolute beginning, but rather continually discover that we have always already begun:

> The explication of the essence of finitude required for the establishment of metaphysics must itself always basically be finite and never absolute. It follows that this reflection on finitude, which is always to be renewed, cannot succeed by exchanging and always adjusting various points of view in order finally and in spite of everything to give us an absolute knowledge of

finitude, a knowledge which is surreptitiously posited as being "true in itself."[30]

There are important consequences for the nature of philosophical questioning which result from this. Such questions cannot honestly seek a definite terminus, as if some fact (or essence) could be uncovered which in principle could not be doubted or questioned. To place something outside the circle of questioning, outside the hermeneutic circle, is to banish it from the domain of meaning. Philosophical questions cannot tend toward the final establishment (*Stiftung*) of a foundation whose full presence insures that no external horizons, no unfulfilled intuitions, remain. Philosophical questioning, the questioning of the meaning of Being as that which determines entities as entities, works with a different scheme of intelligibility and meaning, a *hermeneutic* scheme. The movement of philosophical interpretation (*Auslegung*), grounded hermeneutically in the conditions for questioning Being, moves within a temporal and historical horizon, a horizon which makes possible meaning.

Michael Gelven, in this vein, draws a distinction between an investigation and an inquiry.[31] An investigation is a form of questioning which aims at some definite answer. It terminates when the fact to which it addressed itself is revealed. Such questioning, we might say, is ontic in nature. Investigations can vary in complexity from the most rudimentary questions about the time of day or what to wear, to the level of the natural and social sciences. But all such questions are able to result in a "knowledge" just insofar as the prior ontological understanding involved is itself not brought into question. Inquiries, on the other hand, look to the ontological presuppositions which make possible some ontic mode of conduct, including ontic questioning (investigations). Therefore, inquiries are of a hermeneutic nature. They constitute genuine philosophical questioning.

For Heidegger, man is always already philosophical in his preontological understanding of Being. There is no chasm between a natural and a philosophical attitude. In radicalizing this understanding we do not step outside of it but penetrate deeper into it. Being-in-the-World, then, is the final whole, the necessary beginning, but is in no way absolute. What it nourishes, what it *founds*, is the possibility for continual questioning. We thus conclude much the way Heidegger does:

> Indeed, the question which was raised long ago, is still, and always will be, and which always baffles us, is "What is Being?"[32]

Notes

Introduction

1. Martin Heidegger, *Being and Time*, trans. by John Macquarrie and Edward Robinson (New York: Harper & Row, 1962), 489.

2. Martin Heidegger, *On Time and Being*, trans. by John Stambaugh (New York: Harper & Row, 1972), 78.

3. Ernst Tugendhat, *Der Wahrheitsbegriff bei Husserl und Heidegger* (Berlin: Walter de Gruyter and Company, 1967).

4. Heidegger, *Being and Time*, 60.

5. Ibid., 61.

6. Iso Kern, *Husserl und Kant* (The Hague: Martinus Nijhoff, 1964).

7. Ibid., 196–97.

Chapter 1

1. A succinct formulation of this kind of position can be found in Leszek Kolakowski's *Husserl and the Search for Certitude* (New Haven: Yale University Press, 1975).

2. This concern for ordinary experiential life immediately sets Husserl's phenomenology apart from Kantianism, where scientific cognition is taken as the point of initiation for philosophical reflection. See, for example, Hans-Georg Gadamer, *Philosophical Hermeneutics*, trans. and ed. by David Linge (Berkeley: University of California Press, 1976), 152.

3. While it is true that "Philosophy as Rigorous Science" (1910–11) precedes *Ideas I* historically, and that certain concepts from the *Logical Investigations* are presented in Section I of *Ideas I*, there is no appeal to a structural, scientific ideal in the development of the fundamental phenomenological outlook in the argument of Section II.

4. Edmund Husserl, *Ideas: General Introduction to Pure Phenomenology*, trans. by W.R. Boyce Gibson, Muirhead Library of Philosophy (New York: Humanities Press, 1967), 103. (This work is customarily cited as *Ideas I*.)

5. Eugen Fink, "The Phenomenological Philosophy of Edmund Husserl and Contemporary Crticism" in *The Phenomenology of Husserl: Selected Critical Readings*, trans. and ed. by R.O. Elveton (Chicago: Quandrangle Books, 1970).

6. Ibid., 102.

7. Ibid., 105.

8. These norms, in contrast, for example, to Kant, extend even to formal logic itself; and hence it too needs a foundation.

9. Edmund Husserl, *Cartesian Meditations*, trans. by Dorion Cairns (The Hague: Martinus Nijhoff, 1970), 25–26.

10. Cf. Gaston Berger, *The Cogito in Husserl's Philosophy*, trans. by K. McLaughlin (Evanston: Northwestern University Press, 1972), Chap. 5. Also cf. Robert Sokolowski, *The Formation of Husserl's Concept of Constitution* (The Hague: Martinus Nijhoff, 1964), Chap. 6.

11. It is evident that the word "sees" is used only analogically here, referring to all types of meaningful apprehension.

12. Husserl, *Ideas I*, 85.

13. Fink, "The Phenomenological Philosophy of Husserl," 103.

14. Ibid.

15. This analogy with Hegel should not be pressed, however, for there is not a necessary, dialectical logic in Husserl underlying the movement between the stages.

16. See, for example, Quentin Lauer, *The Triumph of Subjectivity* (New York: Fordham University Press, 1958), 48: "it was necessary to develop precisely those techniques which would enable the subject to eliminate . . . those elements of contingency which make doubt possible." Lauer sees purification from contingency as the essence of the problem.

17. Husserl, *Ideas I*, 106.

18. Ibid., 51.

19. Ibid., 52.

20. Ibid., 51–52

21. Ibid., 117: "jedes Erfassen ist ein Herausfassen."

22. Ibid., 102.

23. Ibid., 107.

24. Ibid., 66–69.

25. Ibid., 212.

26. Edmund Husserl, *The Idea of Phenomenology*, trans. by William Alston and George Nakhnikian (The Hague: Martinus Nijhoff, 1964), 18.

27. Husserl, *Ideas I*, 112.

28. Edmund Husserl, "Phenomenology," trans. by Richard Palmer, *Journal of the British Society for Phenomenology*, II No. 2 (May, 1971), 81.

29. We later realize, of course, that the notion of a limitation is inappropriate, for in transcendental subjectivity, Husserl claims, we discover the whole.

30. See above, p. 13.

31. Husserl, *Ideas I*, 117.

32. Ibid., 119–21.

33. Ibid., 123.

34. Ibid., 72–74.

35. Ibid., 125–26.

36. Ibid., 124.

37. Ibid., 125.

38. Ibid.

39. Ibid., 126.

40. Ibid.

41. Ibid.

42. Emmanuel Levinas, *The Theory of Intuition in Husserl's Phenomenology*, trans. by Andre Orianne (Evanston: Northwestern University Press, 1973), 24.

43. Husserl, *Ideas I*, 137. See also Edmund Husserl, "Philosophy as Rigorous Science," in *Phenomenology and the Crisis of Philosophy*, trans. and ed. by Quentin Lauer (New York: Harper & Row, 1965), 104–06.

44. Husserl, *Ideas I*, 144.

45. Ibid.

46. Ibid., 141–42.

47. Ibid., 140.

48. Ibid., 125.

49. See, for example, Edmund Husserl, *Formal and Transcendental Logic*, trans by Dorion Cairns (The Hague: Martinus Nijohff, 1969), 283–90.

50. Husserl, *Ideas I*, 141.

51. Ibid.

52. Ibid., 143.

53. Ibid., 152.

54. Ibid., 169.

55. The meaning of the transcendental will be the guiding theme of Chapters 2 and 3.

56. Husserl, *Ideas I*, 212.

57. See above, p. 13.

58. See above, p. 15. See also Husserl, "Philosophy as Rigorous Science," 79.

Chapter 2

1. Husserl, *Cartesian Meditations*, 1.

2. Ibid., 4.

3. Ibid., 1.

4. See, for example, Husserl's "Vienna Lecture" in *The Crisis of European Sciences and Transcendental Phenomenology*, trans. by David Carr (Evanston:

Northwestern University Press, 1970), Appendix I. (In future references, this work will be cited merely as *Crisis*.)

5. See Herbert Spiegelberg *The Phenomenological Movement*, 2 vols. (The Hague: Martinus Nijhoff, 1976), I: 75–91.

6. Husserl, *Cartesian Meditations*, 2.

7. The phenomenological *epoche*, in contrast to what might be termed the Socratic one, claims not only to suspend cultural sources of authority, but the universally human acceptance horizon of world belief.

8. See, for example, Part III of Descartes' *Discourse on Method*.

9. Husserl, *Cartesian Meditations*, 2.

10. Ibid.

11. Ibid., 3.

12. Descartes, *Rules for the Direction of the Mind*, in *The Philosophical Works of Descartes*, trans. and ed. by Haldane and Ross, 2 vols. (London: Cambridge University Press, 1970), I: 10.

13. Aristotle *Nichomachean Ethics* 1097b7.

14. Husserl, *Ideas I*, 28.

15. Ibid.

16. Husserl, "Vienna Lecture," 283.

17. See Husserl, *Cartesian Meditations*, 57.

18. Husserl, "Philosophy as Rigorous Science," 140.

19. See Husserl, *Formal and Transcendental Logic*, 158–62.

20. See, for example Husserl's "Philosophy as Rigorous Science." "For the sake of time we must not sacrifice eternity; in order to alleviate our need, we have no right to bequeath to our posterity need upon need as an eventually ineradicable evil" (141). Also, with regard to the task of science: "These men who set their goals in the finite . . . are in no way called to this task" (143).

21. Husserl, *Crisis*, p. 299.

22. Ibid.

23. Husserl, *Cartesian Meditations*, p. 2.

24. Ibid., 9.

25. Ibid.

26. Ibid., 10.

27. Ibid.

28. Ibid.

29. Ibid., 11.

30. For the importance of the structures of presence and absence in all of Husserl's thought, see Robert Sokolowski, *Husserlian Meditations* (Evanston: Northwestern University Press, 1974), Chapter 2. Also, cf. his "Ontological Possibilities in Phenomenology: The Dyad and the One," *The Review of Metaphysics*, 29 (June, 1976), 691–701.

31. This sense of identity, therefore, functions as the foundation for both truth *and* falsity. The latter too can only arise through it. If there were no "intended" identity, no cancellation would be possible.

32. Paul Ricoeur, *Husserl: An Analysis of His Phenomenology.* trans. by Edward Ballard and Lester Embree (Evanston: Northwestern University Press, 1976), 86.

33. For a discussion of the historical background of this idea in nineteenth century epistemology, see Marvin Farber's "The Ideal of a Presuppositionless Philosophy" in *Phenomenology: The Philosophy of Edmund Husserl and Its Interpretations,* ed. by Joseph Kockelman (New York: Doubleday and Company, 1967.

34. Husserl, *Cartesian Meditations*, 13.

35. Ibid.

36. Sokolowski, *Husserlian Meditations*, 31.

37. Edmund Husserl, *Experience and Judgment*, trans. by James Churchill and Karl Ameriks (Evanston: Northwestern University Press, 1973), 25.

38. Ibid., 11.

39. Husserl, *Cartesian Meditations*, 11–14.

40. Ibid., 12.

41. Ibid., 14.

42. Ibid., 13.

43. Husserl, *Ideas I*, 92.

44. Ibid.

45. See Husserl, *Logical Investigations*, trans. by J.N. Findlay, 2 vols. (New York: Humanities Press, 1970), 263–66. Cf. Iso Kern, *Husserl und Kant*, 197.

46. Husserl, *Cartesian Meditations*, 12.

47. Ibid.

48. Ibid., 14.

49. Ibid.

50. Ibid.

51. Ibid., 16.

52. Ibid., 14.

53. Ibid., 16.

54. Ibid., 17.

55. Ibid.

56. Kern, *Husserl und Kant*, 196.

57. See, for example, Robert Sokolowski, *The Formation of Husserl's Concept of Constitution*, 219. "Reality is rejected because it is only presumptive, while consciousness, and consciousness alone, is accepted as a philosophical principle, because it alone, claims Husserl, is apodictically . . . given."

58. This type of question is raised, for example, by Klaus Hartmann in "Abstraction and Existence in Husserl's Phenomenological Reduction," *The Journal of the British Society for Phenomenology*, 2 no. 1 (January, 1971): 15.

59. Husserl, *Cartesian Meditations*, 17.

60. Ibid.
61. Ibid., 17–18.
62. Ibid., 18.
63. Ibid.
64. Ibid.
65. Ibid.
66. Ibid.
67. See Robert Sokolowski, *The Formation of Husserl's Concept of Constitution*, 201: "We find that Husserl uses constitution as the way of expressing the relationship between absolutes and relatives."
68. See above, p. 41.
69. Cf. Husserl's criticism of the Cartesian way to the reduction in the *Crisis*, 155: "it leads to transcendental subjectivity in one leap, as it were, it brings this ego into view as apparently empty of content. . . ."
70. Husserl, *Cartesian Meditations*, 21.
71. Ibid.
72. Husserl, *Crisis*, 178.
73. Husserl, *Cartesian Meditations*, 22.
74. Ibid., p. 23.
75. Ibid., 27.
76. See Kant, *Critique of Pure Reason*, Preface to B edition.
77. For this sense of the apodictic, see *Ideas I*, 60–61.
78. See, for example, Ludwig Landgrebe, "Husserl's Departure from Cartesianism," in *The Phenomenology of Husserl*, ed. by R.O. Elveton, 261.

Chapter 3

1. Gadamer, "The Phenomenological Movement," in *Philosophical Hermeneutics*, 146.
2. Edmund Husserl, *Erste Philosophie: Zweiter Teil* (The Hague: Martinus Nijhoff, 1959), 4.
3. Husserl, *Ideas I*, 212–14.
4. Husserl, *Cartesian Meditations*, 26.
5. Husserl, *Logical Investigations*, 49.
6. Ibid., 435.
7. Ibid.
8. Ibid., 433.
9. Ibid., 436.
10. Ibid., 467.
11. Ibid., 463.
12. Ibid., 465.
13. Ibid.
14. Ibid., 467.

15. Husserl, *Formal and Transcendental Logic*, 78–79.
16. Husserl, *Logical Investigations*, 476.
17. Ibid.
18. Ibid., 477.
19. Ibid., 468.
20. Husserl, *Experience and Judgment*, 133.
21. Ibid., 134.
22. For the importance of the genus "extension" in the domain of wholes and parts, see Thomas Seebohm, "Reflexion and Totality in the Philosophy of Husserl," *Journal of the British Society for Phenomenology*, 4, No. 1 (January, 1973): 23.
23. Husserl, *Ideas I*, 52–53.
24. Husserl, *Logical Investigations*, 443.
25. See, for example, *Ideas I*, 82–85 and 95–97. Also, cf. *Cartesian Meditations*, 11–14.
26. Husserl, *Ideas I*, 93–95.
27. Husserl, *Experience and Judgment*, 136.
28. Husserl, *Ideas I*, 152.
29. Husserl, *Logical Investigations*, 445.
30. Ibid., 439.
31. Ibid.
32. Ibid., 445.
33. Ibid., 443.
34. Ibid.
35. Ibid., 445.
36. Ibid.
37. Ibid.
38. Husserl, *Ideas I*, 152.
39. Ibid., 154.
40. Ibid., 156.
41. Husserl, *Cartesian Meditations*, 84.
42. See, for example, Roman Ingarden, *On the Motives Which Led Husserl to Transcendental Idealism*, trans. by Arnor Hannibalsson (The Hague: Martinus Nijhoff, 1975), pt. 1.
43. See Spiegelberg, *The Phenomenological Movement*, 168–72.
44. The natural attitude is a transcendental concept first introduced explicitly in 1907 in *The Idea of Phenomenology*.
45. Husserl, *Formal and Transcendental Logic*, 153.
46. Ibid., 152.
47. See above, p. 164.
48. Husserl, *Experience and Judgment*, 137.
49. Here we have a basic equivocation on the sense of "world" in Husserl's thought, one which will prove of the utmost importance in relation to Heidegger's view of phenomenology.

50. Husserl, *Experience and Judgment*, 138.
51. Ibid.
52. This is the notion of "world form" in *Ideas I*.
53. Friedrich Nietzsche, *The Gay Science*, trans. by Walter Kaufmann (New York: Random House, 1974), 167.
54. Husserl, *Formal and Transcendental Logic*, 154–55.
55. Ibid., 165: "Consequently a certain *ideality* lies in the sense of every experienceable object, including every physical object . . . . It is the universal ideality of all intentional unities over against the multiplicities constituting them."
56. Husserl, *Logical Investigations*, 445.
57. Husserl, *Ideas I*, 212.
58. Husserl, "Phenomenology," 87.
59. Husserl, *Crisis*, Appendix IV.
60. Husserl, *Ideas I*, 92.
61. Husserl, "Phenomenology," 89.
62. Ibid., 86.
63. This is an important difference, for example, between Husserl's transcendental idealism and that of Kant and Fichte.
64. Husserl, "Phenomenology," 86.
65. The concrete stream of experience is apprehended "after the fashion of an Idea in the Kantian sense." (*Ideas I*, 240.)
66. Husserl, *Crisis*, 189. Thus Husserl might well agree with Heidegger that the "scandal of philosophy" consists not so much in an inability to prove the existence of the external world, but in the recurrent demand for such a proof.
67. Eugen Fink, "Husserl's Phenomenology and Contemporary Criticism," 95.
68. Husserl, "Phenomenology," 88.

Chapter 4

1. See Sokolowski, *Husserlian Meditations*, 170.
2. Husserl, *Ideas I*, 241.
3. See Husserl, "Phenomenology," 78–80.
4. Franz Brentano, *Psychology from an Empirical Standpoint*, trans. by O. Kraus and L. McAlister (New York: Humanities Press, 1973). Also, cf. Spiegelberg, *The Phenomenological Movement*, 36–42.
5. See Joseph Kockelmans, *Edmund Husserl's Phenomenological Psychology* (Pittsburgh: Duguesne University Press, 1967), 67–71.
6. Spiegelberg, *The Phenomenological Movement*, 40.
7. Ibid., 107–15. Also, cf. Husserl, *Ideas I*, 249–50; "Philosophy as Rigorous Science," 91; *Logical Investigations*, 552–60; and *Crisis*, 233–34.

8. Husserl, *Cartesian Meditations*, 33.

9. Husserl, *Ideas I*, 115.

10. In this regard, Levinas suggests that the absence of the ego as pole of identity in the *Logical Investigations* testifies to Husserl's attempt to overcome such a conception of the self. (*The Theory of Intuition*, chap. 1.)

11. Husserl, *Cartesian Meditations*, 33.

12. See, for example, the *Logical Investigations*, 553. This in turn implies the inseparability of *hyle* and *morphe*, as well as the impossibility of a consciousness without a world, clarifying certain ambiguities found in *Ideas I*.

13. Husserl, "Philosophy as Rigorous Science," 79.

14. Ibid., 100. See also, *Crisis*, 21–23.

15. Husserl, "Philosophy as Rigorous Science," 102. See also, "Phenomenology," 81. Heidegger makes a similar point in *Being and Time*, 28–31.

16. Husserl, "Philosophy as Rigorous Science," 95.

17. Husserl, "Phenomenology," 81.

18. Husserl, *Logical Investigations*, 557.

19. Aron Gurwitsch, "On the Intentionality of Consciousness" in *Phenomenology*, ed. by Joseph Kockelmans, 130.

20. Ibid.

21. Husserl, *Logical Investigations*, 559.

22. Husserl, "Phenomenology," 79.

23. Husserl, *Crisis*, 234.

24. Husserl, "Phenomenology," 80.

25. Ibid.

26. Husserl, *Cartesian Meditations*, 32.

27. Husserl, "Phenomenology," 83.

28. Ibid.

29. Edmund Husserl, *The Paris Lectures*, trans. by Peter Koestenbaum (The Hague: Martinus Nijhoff, 1964), 30.

30. Kockelmans, *Edmund Husserl's Phenomenological Psychology*, 258.

31. Husserl, *Crisis*, 183.

32. Fink, "Husserl's Phenomenology and Contemporary Criticism," 95.

33. Husserl, *Cartesian Meditations*, 62.

34. Ibid., 63.

35. This appears in vol. 9 of *Husserliana*, 256–63. It appears in English translation in *New Scholasticism*, 44 (1970): 334–44.

36. Ibid., 335 in English translation.

37. Ibid., 336.

38. The inadequacy of the term "consciousness" for the reference to the self by Heidegger, however, soon becomes clear.

39. Spiegelberg, *The Phenomenological Movement.*, 280.

40. See the *Cartesian Meditations*, 26.

41. Husserl, "Phenomenology," 87.

42. Spiegelberg, *The Phenomenological Movement*, 281.

43. Alwin Diemer, *Edmund Husserl* (Meisenheim am Glan: Verlag Anton Hain, 1965), 19–20.

44. Ibid., 20.

45. See Joseph Kockelmans, "Husserl's Phenomenological Philosophy in the Light of Contemporary Criticism," *Phenomenology*, ed. by Kockelmans, 229: "Heidegger's intentional analysis can never take the form of constitutive analysis."

46. See Spiegelberg, *The Phenomenological Movement*, 124. See also Tugendhat, *Der Wahrheitsbegriff bei Husserl und Heidegger*, 262.

47. Heidegger, *Being and Time*, 75.

48. Diemer, *Edmund Husserl*, 20.

49. *Husserliana*, Volume IX, 602.

50. Husserl, "Phenomenology," 81.

51. *Husserliana*, vol. 9, 602.

52. Heidegger, *Being and Time*, 60.

53. Ibid., 25.

54. Ibid., 24.

55. Ibid.

56. Ibid., 25.

57. Paul Ricoeur gives a nice treatment of this hermeneutic of the "I am" in contrast to the Cartesian *cogito* in "The Critique of Subjectivity and *Cogito* in the Philosophy of Heidegger," *Heidegger and the Quest for Truth*, ed. by M. Frings (Chicago: Quadrangle Books, 1968), 62–74.

58. Heidegger, *Being and Time*, 195.

59. Ibid.

60. Ibid., 27.

61. Martin Heidegger, *Kant and the Problem of Metaphysics*, trans. by James Churchill (Bloomington: Indiana University Press, 1972), 81.

62. Martin Heidegger, *The Essence of Reasons*, trans. by T. Malick (Evanston: Northwestern University Press, 1969), 97.

63. Ibid., 29.

64. Ibid., 37–39.

65. Ibid., 39.

66. Ibid., 41.

67. Husserl, *Ideas I*, 52.

68. Cf. Joseph Kockelmans, *The World in Science and Philosophy* (Milwaukee: Bruce Publishing Co., 1969), 55–72.

69. Sokolowski, *Husserlian Meditations*, 170.

70. Husserl, *Crisis*, 143.

71. We shall capitalize the term "world" whenever referring to Heidegger's usage, while leaving the lower case for the Husserlian meaning. In addition, "world[1]" will signify the notion of the totality of beings, "world[2]" the horizon which bestows upon them their Being.

72. Husserl, *Crisis*, 143.

73. Husserl, *Cartesian Meditations*, 62.

74. See Walter Biemal, *Martin Heidegger: An Illustrated Study*, trans. by J.L. Metha (New York: Harcourt, Brace, Jovanovich, 1976), 41.

75. Heidegger, *Being and Time*, 92–93.

76. Ibid., 105.

77. Ibid., 119–22.

78. Ibid.

79. Heidegger's thinking, at this stage, seems to be tending toward an identification of World and Being. The function of the World, when no longer limited to the environmental world (*Umwelt*), but extended to embrace all possible worlds, as the ultimate horizon of meaning, as that upon the basis of which beings can be, seems to parallel the wholistic and foundational nature of Being itself. Caution, however, should be exercised here. The World is a moment in the essential unity of Being-in-the-World, that is, in the Being of Dasein. An outright identification of Being and World would thus seem to fail to do justice to the nature of Being in relation to man. The World functions as the locus or place of Being, the "There" (*da*) of Being. This does not resolve the issue, which may remain problematic in Heidegger, but perhaps points the way to an understanding of the later development of Heidegger's thought. See Kockelmans, *The World in Science and Philosophy*, pp. 69–72; and William Richardson, *Heidegger: From Phenomenology to Thought* (The Hague: Martinus Nijhoff, 1974), 55–58 and 623–28.

80. Heidegger, *Kant and the Problem of Metaphysics*, 250.

81. Heidegger, *Being and Time*, 107.

82. Ibid., 254.

83. Husserl, *Cartesian Meditations*, par. 32 et passim.

84. Joseph Kockelmans, *A First Introduction to Husserl's Phenomenology* (Pittsburgh: Duquesne University Press, 1967), 215.

85. Husserl, *Cartesian Meditations*, 68.

86. Heidegger, *The Essence of Reasons*, 29. Cf. *Kant and the Problem of Metaphysics*, 243.

87. Martin Heidegger, *Die Grundprobleme der Phänomenologie* (Frankfurt am Main: Vittorio Klostermann, 1975), 82: "It is grounded ontologically in the basic constitution of Dasein."

88. Ibid., 100–01.

89. Ibid., 102. Cf. Richardson's discussion of the fragmentary nature of a conception of man as a "subject of acts" in "The Unconscious in Heidegger," *Review of Existential Psychology and Psychiatry*, 4 (1965): 265–90.

90. Heidegger, *Being and Time*, 73.

91. Ibid.

92. Ibid., 251.

93. Sokolowski, *Husserlian Meditations*, 204: "The world and world-belief are nested, respectively, within being and being-belief, and man is the being that has a world because being appears to him."

94. Husserl, *Formal and Transcendental Logic*, 158.

95. Husserl, *Logical Investigations*, 765.

96. This is a quotation taken from the lecture notes of a seminar given by Heidegger in 1924, taken by Helene Wess, and cited by Tugendhat in *Der Wahrheitsbegriff bei Husserl und Heidegger*, 262.

97. While there is no explicit reference to Descartes or Husserl in these passages, the positions presented make it evident that Heidegger has them in mind.

98. Heidegger, *Being and Time*, 367.

99. Kockelmans, "Husserl's Phenomenological Philosophy in the Light of Contemporary Criticism," 225–26.

Chapter 5

1. Berger, *The Cogito in Husserl's Philosophy*, 5.

2. Kolakowski, *Husserl and the Search for Certitude*, 5.

3. Aristotle *Metaphysics* 1005b.

4. Eugen Fink, "Vergegenwärtigung und Bild," *Jahrbuch für Philosophie und phänomenologische Forschung*, 11 (1930): 279.

5. Husserl, *Crisis*, Appendix 9.

6. Fink, "Husserl's Phenomenology and Contemporary Criticism," 95.

7. Ibid.

8. See above, chap. 4, p. 87.

9. See Otto Pöggeler, *Der Denkweg Martin Heideggers* (Pfulligen: Neske, 1963), 72.

10. Kant, *Critique of Pure Reason*, B19.

11. Ibid., A12, B25.

12. Husserl, *Crisis*, pars. 27–32.

13. Hegel, *The Phenomenology of Spirit*, trans. by Ballie (New York: Harper & Row, 1967), 130–31.

14. Rudolph Boehm, "Husserl's Concept of the Absolute" in *The Phenomenology of Husserl*, ed. by R.O. Elveton, 174–201.

15. Husserl, *Ideas I*, 138.

16. See above, chap. 1, p. 22.

17. Gadamer, *Philosophical Hermeneutics*, 121.

18. Heidegger, *The Essence of Reasons*, 29.

19. Aristotle *Physics* 219b1.

20. See Heidegger, *Kant and the Problem of Metaphysics*, 223: "Where there is a question concerning a power and one delimits its possibilities, there is at the same time a non-power (*Nicht-Konnen*). An omnipotent being need

not ask, 'What am I able to do?'; i.e., 'What am I not able to do?' Whosoever asks 'What am I able to do?' betrays thereby his own finitude. And whosoever is concerned in his innermost interests by such a question reveals a finitude in his innermost nature.

21. Ibid., 226.
22. Ibid., 244.
23. Ibid., 238.
24. See Kant, *Critique of Pure Reason*, A20, B34.
25. Heidegger, *Kant and the Problem of Metaphysics*, 31.
26. Ibid., 32.
27. Ibid., 237.
28. Ibid., 236.
29. Hans-Georg Gadamer, *Truth and Method*, trans. by Barden and Cumming (New York: The Seabury Press, 1975), 234.
30. Heidegger, *Kant and the Problem of Metaphysics*, 245.
31. Michael Gelven, *Winter, Friendship, and Guilt: The Sources of Self-Inquiry* (New York: Harper & Row, 1972), 6–10.
32. Aristotle *Metaphysics* 1028b2.

Selected Bibliography

Berger, Gaston. *The Cogito in Husserl's Philosophy*. Translated by Kathleen McLaughlin. Evanston: Northwestern University Press, 1972.

Biemel, Walter. "The Decisive Phase in the Development of Husserl's Philosophy." *The Phenomenology of Husserl: Selected Critical Readings*. Edited by R.O. Elveton. Chicago: Quadrangle Books, 1970.

————. "Husserls Encyclopaedia Britannica Artikel und Heideggers Anmerkungen dazu." *Tijdschrift voor Philosophie*, XII (1950), 246–280.

————. *Martin Heidegger: An Illustrated Study*. Translated by J.L. Metha. New York: Harcourt, Brace, Jovanovich, 1976.

Boehm, Rudolph. "Basic Reflections on Husserl's Phenomenological Reduction." Translated by Q. Lauer. *International Philosophical Quarterly*, V, No. 2 (May, 1965), 183–202.

————. "Husserl's Concept of the Absolute." Translated by R.O. Elveton. *The Phenomenology of Husserl: Selected Critical Readings*. Edited by R.O. ELveton. Chicago: Quadrangle Books, 1970.

Brand, Gerd. "Intentionality, Reduction and Intentional Analysis in Husserl's Later Manuscripts." Translated by Joseph J. Kockelmans. *Phenomenology: The Philosophy of Edmund Husserl and Its Interpretation*. Edited by Joseph J. Kockelmans. New York: Doubleday and Company, 1967.

————. *Welt, Ich, und Zeit*. The Hague: Martinus Nijhoff, 1955.

Brentano, Franz. *Psychology from an Empirical Standpoint*. Translated by O. Kraus and L. McAlister. New York: The Humanities Press, 1973.

Chisholm, Roderick M., ed. *Realism and the Background of Phenomenology*. Glencoe: The Free Press, 1960.

Descartes, Rene. *The Philosophical Works of Descartes*. Translated by Elizabeth S. Haldane and G.R.T. Ross. 2 vols. Cambridge: The Cambridge University Press, 1970.

Diemer, Alwin. *Edmund Husserl*. Meisenheim am Glan: Anton Hain, 1965.

Farber, Marvin. *The Foundations of Phenomenology*. Cambridge, Mass.: Harvard University Press, 1943.

Farber, Marvin. "The Ideal of a Presuppositionless Philosophy." *Phenomenology: The Philosophy of Edmund Husserl and Its Interpretation*. Edited by Joseph J. Kockelmans. New York: Doubleday and Company, 1967.

Fink, Eugen. "The Phenomenological Philosophy of Edmund Husserl and Contemporary Criticism." Translated by R.O. Elveton. *The Phenomenology of Husserl: Selected Critical Readings*. Edited by R.O. Elveton. Chicago: Quadrangle Books, 1970.

————. "Vergegenwärtigung und Bild." *Jahrbuch für Philosophie und phänomenologische Forschung*, XI (1930), 239–310.

————. "What Does the Phenomenology of Edmund Husserl Want to Accomplish? Translated by A. Grugan. *Research in Phenomenology*, II (1972), 5–27.

Gadamer, Hans-Georg. *Philosophical Hermeneutics*. Translated and edited by David E. Linge. Berkeley: University of California Press, 1976.

————. "The Problem of Historical Consciousness." Translated by Jeff L. Close. *Graduate Faculty Philosophy Journal*, V. No. 1 (Fall, 1975), 8–52.

————. *Truth and Method*. Translated by G. Barden and J. Cumming. New York: The Seabury Press, 1975.

Gelven, Michael. *A Commentary on Heidegger's "Being and Time."* New York: Harper and Row, 1970.

————. *Winter, Friendship, and Guilt: The Sources of Self-Inquiry*. New York: Harper and Row, 1972.

Gurwitsch, Aron. *The Field of Consciousness*. Pittsburgh: Duguesne University Press, 1964.

————. "On the Intentionality of Consciousness." *Phenomenology: The Philosophy of Edmund Husserl and Its Interpretation*. Edited by Joseph J. Kockelmans. New York: Doubleday and Company, 1967.

————. *Studies in Phenomenology and Psychology*. Evanston: Northwestern University Press, 1966.

Hartmann, Klaus. "Abstraction and Existence in Husserl's Phenomenological Reduction." *The Journal of the British Society for Phenomenology*, II, No. 1 (Ja. '71), 10–18.

Hegel, G.W.F. *The Phenomenology of Mind*. Translated by J.B. Baillie. Harper and Row, 1967.

Heidegger, Martin. *Being and Time*. Translated by J. Macquarrie and E. Robinson. New York: Harper and Row, 1962.

————. *The Essence of Reasons*. Translated by T. Malick. Evanston: Northwestern University Press, 1969.

————. *Die Grundprobleme der Phänomenologie*. Frankfurt am Main: Vittorio Klostermann, 1975.

————. "The Idea of Phenomenology." Translated by J. Neely and J.A. Novak. *New Scholasticism*, XLIV, No. 3 (Summer, 1970), 325–344.

————. *Kant and the Problem of Metaphysics*. Translated by James Churchill. Bloomington: Indiana Univesity Press, 1972.

————. *On Time and Being*. Translated by Joan Stambaugh. New York: Harper and Row, 1972.

————. *What is a Thing?* Translated by W.B. Barton and Vera Deutsch. Chicago: Henry Regnery Company, 1967.

Husserl, Edmund. *Cartesian Meditations*. Translated by Dorion Cairns. The Hague: Martinus Nijhoff, 1970.

————. *The Crisis of European Sciences and Transcendental Phenomenology*. Translated by David Carr. Evanston: Northwestern University Press, 1970.

————. *Erste Philosophie*. Edited by R. Boehm. 2 vols. *Husserliana* VII, VIII. The Hague, Martinus Nijhoff, 1956, 1959.

————. *Experience and Judgment*. Translated by James Churchill and K. Ameriks. Evanston: Northwestern University Press, 1973.

————. *Formal and Transcendental Logic*. Translated by Dorion Cairns. The Hague: Martinus Nijhoff, 1969.

————. *The Idea of Phenomenology*. Translated by W.P. Alston and G. Nakhnikian. The Hague: Martinus Nijhoff, 1964.

————. *Ideas: General Introduction to Pure Phenomenology*. Translated by W.R. Boyce Gibson. New York: The Humanities Press, 1967.

————*Logical Investigations*. Translated by J. N.Findlay. 2 vols. New York: The Humanities Press, 1970.

Husserl Edmund. *The Paris Lectures*. Translated by P. Koestenbaum. The Hague: Martinus Nijhoff, 1964.

————. "Phenomenology." Translated by Richard Palmer. *Journal of the British Society for Phenomenology*, II, No. 2 (May, 1971), 77–90.

————. "Phenomenology and Anthropology." Translated by R.G. Schmitt. *Realism and the Background of Phenomenology.* Edited by R. Chisholm. Glencoe: The Free Press, 1967.

————. *The Phenomenology of Internal Time-Consciousness.* Translated by J. Churchill. Bloomington: Indiana University Press, 1964.

————. "Philosophy as Rigorous Science." Translated by Q. Lauer. *Phenomenology and the Crisis of Philosophy.* Edited by Q. Lauer, New York: Harper and Row, 1965.

Ingarden, Roman. *On the Motives Which Led Husserl to Transcendental Idealism.* Translated by Arnor Hannibalsson. The Hague: Martinus Nijhoff, 1975.

Kant, Immanuel. *The Critique of Pure Reason.* Translated by Norman Kemp Smith. New York: St. Martin's Press, 1965.

Kern, Iso. *Husserl und Kant.* The Hague: Martinus Nijhoff, 1964.

Kockelmans, Joseph. *Edmund Husserl: An Introduction to His Phenomenology.* Pittsburgh: Duquesne University Press, 1967.

————. *Edmund Husserl's Phenomenological Psychology.* Pittsburgh: Duquesne University Press, 1967.

————. *Martin Heidegger: A First Introduction to His Philosophy.* Pittsburgh: Duquesne University Press, 1965.

————. *Phenomenology: The Philosophy of Edmund Husserl and Its Interpretation.* New York: Doubleday and Company, 1967.

————. "Phenomenologico-Psychological and Transcendental Reductions in Husserl's *Crisis.*" *Analecta Husserliana.* Edited by A. Tymieniecka. Vol. II (1972), pp. 78–89.

————. "World Constitution: Reflections on Husserl's Transcendental Idealism." *Analecta Husserliana.* Edited by A. Tymieniecka. Vol. I (1970), pp. 11–35.

Kockelmans, Joseph. *The World in Science and Philosophy.* Milwaukee: The Bruce Publishing Company, 1969.

Kolakowski, Leszek. *Husserl and the Search for Certitude.* New Haven, Yale University Press, 1975.

Kung, Guido. "The Phenomenological Reduction as *Epoche* and as Explication." *Monist*, Vol. 59, No. 1 (January, 1975), 63–80.

Landgrebe, Ludwig. "Husserl's Departure from Cartesianism." *The Phenomenology of Husserl: Selected Critical Readings.* Edited and translated by R.O. Elveton. Chicago: Quadrangle Press, 1970.

————. "The World as a Phenomenological Problem." Translated by D. Cairns. *Philosophy and Phenomenological Research*, I, No. 2 (September, 1940), 38–58.

Lauer, Quentin. *The Triumph of Subjectivity: An Introduction to Transcendental Phenomenology.* New York: Fordham University Press, 1958.

Levinas, Emmanuel. *The Theory of Intuition in Husserl's Phenomenology.* Translated by A. Orianne. Evanston: Northwestern University Press, 1973.

Marx, Werner. *Heidegger and the Tradition.* Translated by T. Kisiel and Murray Greene. Evanston: Northwestern University Press, 1971.

Merleau-Ponty, Maurice. *The Phenomenology of Perception.* Translated by Colin Smith. New York: The Humanities Press, 1962.

Natanson, Maurice. *Edmund Husserl: Philosopher of Infinite Tasks.* Evanston: Northwestern University Press, 1973.

Nietzsche, Friedrich. *The Gay Science.* Translated by Walter Kaufmann. New York: Random House, 1974.

Osborn, A.D. *Edmund Husserl and His Logical Investigations.* Cambridge, Mass.: Edwards Brothers, 1949.

Palmer, Richard. *Hermeneutics.* Evanston: Northwestern University Press, 1969.

Pöggeler, Otto. *Der Denkweg Martin Heidegger.* Pfullingen: Neske, 1963.

Richardson, William. *Heidegger: Through Phenomenology to Thought.* The Hague: Martinus Nijhoff, 1963.

Richardson, William. "The Unconscious in Heidegger." *Review of Existential Psychology and Psychiatry*, IV (1965), 265–290.

Ricoeur, Paul. "The Critique of Subjectivity and *Cogito* in the Philosophy of Heidegger." *Heidegger and the Quest for Truth.* Edited by M. Frings. Chicago: Quadrangle Books, 1968.

————. *Husserl: An Analysis of His Phenomenology.* Translated by E. B. Ballard and L. Embree. Evanston: Northwestern University Press, 1967.

Sallis, John. *Phenomenology and the Return to Beginnings.* Pittsburgh: Duquense University Press, 1973.

Seebohm, Thomas, "Reflexion and Totality in the Philosophy of Husserl." *Journal of the British Society for Phenomenology*, IV, No. 1 (January, 1973), 20–30.

Sokolowski, Robert. *The Formation of Husserl's Concept of Constitution.* The Hague: Martinus Nijhoff, 1964.

————. *Husserlian Meditations*. Evanston: Northwestern University Press, 1974.

————. "Ontological Possibilities in Phenomenology: The Dyad and the One." *The Review of Metaphysics*, XXIX, No. 4 (June 1976), 691–701.

Spiegelberg, Herbert. *The Phenomenological Movement*. 2 vols. The Hague: Martinus Nijhoff, 1965.

————. *Phenomenology in Psychology and Psychiatry*. Evanston: Northwestern University Press, 1972.

Stapleton, Timothy J., "Husserl and Kantianism." *Auslegung*, IV (Fall, 1977), 81–104.

————. "The Logic of Husserl's Transcendental Reduction." *Man and World*, 15/4 (Winter, 1982).

Strasser, Stephan. *Phenomenology and the Human Sciences: A Contribution to a New Scientific Ideal*. Translated by Henry J. Koren. Pittsburgh: Duquense University Press, 1963.

Tugendhat, Ernst. *Der Wahrheitsbegriff bei Husserl und Heidegger*. Berlin: Walter de Gruyter and Company, 1967.

Index

RELATED TITLES FROM SUNY PRESS

PHENOMENOLOGY IN A PLURALISTIC CONTEXT. William L. McBride and Calvin O. Schrag, editors.

PHENOMENOLOGY: DIALOGUES & BRIDGES. William L. McBride and Calvin O. Schrag, editors.

RECONSTRUCTION OF THINKING. Robert C. Neville.

THE SLAYERS OF MOSES. The Emergence of Rabbinic Interpretation in Modern Literary Theory. Susan A. Handelman.

EROS AND IRONY: A Prelude to Philosophical Anarchism. David L. Hall.

THE QUEST FOR WHOLENESS. Carl G. Vaught.

EXISTENTIAL TECHNICS. Don Ihde.

WITTGENSTEIN AND PHENOMENOLOGY: A Comparative Study of the Later Wittgenstein, Husserl, Heidegger, and Merleau-Ponty. Nicholas F. Gier.